WAYS TO RAISE HAPPY, LOVING KIDS *and avoid parent burnout*

Mary Manz Simon

THOMAS NELSON PUBLISHERS
Nashville • Atlanta • London • Vancouver

For Hank
my partner in parenting

1 John 4:12

Published in Nashville, Tennessee, by Thomas Nelson, Inc., Publishers, and distributed in Canada by Word Communications, Ltd., Richmond, British Columbia, and in the United Kingdom by Word (UK), Ltd., Milton Keynes, England.

Scripture quotations are from the NEW KING JAMES VERSION of the Bible. Copyright © 1979, 1980, 1982, Thomas Nelson, Inc., Publishers.

Library of Congress Cataloging-in-Publication Data

Simon, Mary Manz, 1948–
52 ways to raise happy, loving kids / Mary Manz Simon.
    p. cm.
ISBN 0-8407-4037-9
    1. Parenting—Religious aspects—Christianity. 2. Child rearing—Religious aspects—Christianity. 3. Parent and child—Religious aspects—Christianity. I. Title. II. Title: Fifty-two ways to raise happy, loving kids.
BV4529.S435   1993
248.8′6—dc20   93-10780
                                                                            CIP

Printed in the United States of America

3 4 5 6 7 - 99 98 97 96 95

Contents

✖ Introduction

Being a parent: Is it what you expected?

Quite honestly, and perhaps like you, I wasn't sure what parenting would be like.

In some ways, being a parent has been a far more wonderful experience than I anticipated. How could I have known the joy of seeing Angela lead cheers in front of a gymnasium full of screaming students? Or the thrill I felt when Matthew made a game-winning catch in the t-ball game? Or the humility at reading Christy's very correct and appropriate editing of these manuscript pages? Quite possibly like you, I think parenting is wonderful.

But in almost every way, parenting has been more challenging, demanding, and exhausting than I could ever have imagined. Even with my years of knowing better, I've yelled at a child who insists on leaving shoes in the living room. After nine straight days of basketball games, I've complained about driving to yet another after-school activity. And perhaps like you, I reluctantly face the fact that my children are growing up and away from me. I think parenting is tough.

But I've learned and relearned one basic fact: we must maximize the time we have with our children. We must focus on what really counts.

That's why I wrote this book. I wrote this book for the new mother of a four month old, who told me just recently, "I want my daughter to be happy. I want to give her the very best in life."

This book is for the father of three, who drives for four hours just to attend a PTA meeting at his children's school, then drives four hours through the night, back to his home.

This book is for you, because I believe most parents want to be good parents. I believe most parents want to make a difference in the lives of their children.

And I believe this can happen by focusing on what's important. I've chosen 52 aspects of parenting that can help you have a positive impact on your child. There is absolutely no substitute for your time and emotional investment in your child, but reading this book will help you focus that passion for your child into areas of critical importance.

The expectations you've had of yourself as a parent may or may not have already been met. But one expectation can become reality: You can raise a happy, loving child without suffering from parent burnout. By caring enough about your parenting to pick up this book, you've already taken the first step.

1 🦋 Parent with a Purpose

What are your long-term goals as a parent?

You picked up this book, so that simple action revealed at least one goal: You want to raise a happy, loving child without going crazy. You want to eliminate the unnecessary hassles of parenting and focus on what really counts. Those are good goals.

Keystone Activity But can you visualize other aspects of the "big picture" for your parenting? If it's hard to look beyond the daily routines of supervising homework and buying cat food, ask one question: "What is our daily keystone?" Most families have something they do each day. A good keystone activity brings everyone to one place. Do you eat breakfast together? Pray as a family unit? Ride together in the car to school and work? Your individual family keystone can lead you to discover some underlying values. Record your "to-gether-time" activity here:

Parents need to remember what's important. Setting goals will give you something to work toward and a standard against which to measure your progress. These lofty images won't get you to the dentist's office on time or make it easier to accept a D on a child's report card, but goals will help you see the big picture.

Don't Get Sidetracked Parents naturally get sidetracked from time to time. When you're concerned about your daughter's choice of friends or worried about a sick child, you properly focus on the crisis of the moment. But if you parent with a clearly defined purpose, you will always return to the basic issues.

Trends in parenting come along every so often. Personalities in the news and the lack of other newsworthy topics can stimulate media to highlight various aspects of parenting. As a result, certain issues become "hot" for a time. Use such trends to give you a jump-start in a certain issue. For example, if the media emphasizes travel with children, collect the ideas that your family can use in this area.

But don't get sidetracked for long. The basics of effective parenting don't change. Priorities within your list of goals might vary from time to time, and how you meet those goals will change, but what you want for your child and what you want from parenting will remain fairly constant throughout the years.

2 ✺ Plan Places and Spaces

Kids need a lot of "stuff." Provide places that are clearly labeled. Look at varieties of storage options: spaces must be appropriate for everything from wet mittens (dry the mittens on an empty shoe rack) to odd shaped boxed games (underneath hanging clothes in a closet).

Use these ideas to simplify your life, reduce hassles, prevent misplaced items, and save time.

Create Workable Storage Areas Explain to your child how individual storage areas are designed to work. For the first few days after a new area is organized, invest extra time to be physically present while your child puts away things. Here are examples:

Problem: Wheeled toys of all shapes, kinds, and sizes are jammed into the garage.

Solution: Create a parking lot. Ask your child to line up all wheeled toys. Park the one in front that is used most frequently. Tape a masking tape line onto the floor on each side of that toy.

Then do the same thing around other vehicles.

Problem: Children drop backpacks and lunch boxes wherever it's convenient when they come home from school.

Solution: Designate specific storage spaces for outer wear and school items. One parent cut a kitchen pantry in half just to make a kid's closet, with a hanging rack for coats, a shelf for backpacks and lunch boxes, and baskets for hats and mittens. You don't have to go to this extreme, but make sure each child has a specific place for every item.

Reduce, Reuse, Recycle These environmental watchwords can eliminate unnecessary clutter. Let your child help you set up clearly labeled containers that will be a permanent part of your household. Store the containers wherever convenient: under a workbench, in the laundry room, etc. Categories might include:

- thrift shop or garage sale (outgrown clothes, toys that aren't used)
- hand-me-downs (clothes your child received from someone that need to be returned)
- mending (clothes that need repair)

- recycle (broken metal toys to be taken for aluminum recycling, old magazines labeled "cut" for school projects)

Plan Your Child's Personal Space Before you add a swingset, climber, or basketball hoop outdoors, consider the location of overhead wires, light poles, shade trees, and gutters. Play equipment installed near flowering bushes or trees means bees and other flying insects will always be nearby. Add only one piece of equipment at a time. You don't want to lose the biggest asset of outdoor space—a place to run free.

Indoor spaces can be shared, but each child should have a corner, shelf, or hanging rack that belongs just to him. Usage of indoor space will change frequently, so periodically review with your child how the space is working for him. The biggest clean-out times for a family will be before a child's birthday or Christmas. Your child will add new items after these days, so go through existing items before the holiday. Then space will be ready and waiting for the new things. Whenever possible, involve your child in the planning, decorating, and organizing process.

3 🦋 Prepare for the Inevitable

"It's a beautiful day. Let's go to the park!"

"Jaime's basketball team won in the tournament. She gets to play for the championship on Friday!"

"Greg caught his big toe under the screen door. I don't know how it happened, but he's screaming. I've got to take him to the emergency room, fast."

Know the "Givens" Celebrating the spontaneous or coping with completely unexpected happenings is part of parenting. But there are many "givens." Parents can be fairly sure certain things *will* happen. For example:

- "We're going to Grandma's. You know we always go there on her birthday."
- "It's Monday. Did you empty your wastepaper basket for the garbage pickup?"
- "I'm sorry your snowman is gone. After yesterday's bright sun and today's warmer temperatures, I'm not surprised your snowman melted away."

Plan for What's Expected Each parent
will have various "inevitables," and these might
differ for each child. A parent who accurately
says, "If this is the situation, then this will
probably be the result," can prevent potential
problem situations, experience less stress, and
have a greater sense of confidence.

Use the chart below to trigger planning for
your "inevitables." Then think through a "sure
thing" that might involve your child today.
Identify the situation, the probable result, and
the way you can prepare.

The Situation	The Probable Result	How I Can Prepare
Child is getting a cold	Child will use lots of tissues and leave dirty tissues lying all over	Tape a small empty paper sack onto the box of tissues
Day before leaving on family vacation	Child will be wound up and full of energy	Make a list of household jobs he can do independently so he can put excess energy to good use
Going through a turnstile	Child will get hit in the head	Hold him by the hand and manually move turnstile arm

4 🦋 Be a Pro-active Parent

Parents must react immediately in some situations. But often we can take the initiative, or be pro-active, and prevent a situation before it ever happens. Begin to think as a pro-active parent. Get into a regular pattern of *acting in advance* instead of *reacting in response*. Thinking in this way can positively impact your approach to many situations and result in safer, less stressful parenting.

For example: Your child is scheduled for his regular checkup. The doctor is running late. By the time your name is called, your child is hungry, tired, and acting up. Could this situation have been prevented? Probably. Reduce the hassle factor next time: help your child pack a bag of books, toys, and finger snacks.

The point is clear: advance thinking and action pays off in smoother, more enjoyable, safer parenting. This frees you to invest your emotional energy in your child, instead of in picking up the pieces in various situations.

A pro-active parent can prevent injury, embarrassment, and hassle in some classic problem situations illustrated below. Once you think as a pro-active parent, you'll continually revise your own mental list of ways to prevent these kinds of problems.

"Wait until I'm off the phone." You've been there: you're talking on the phone and your child acts up. Be pro-active:

- Get a long, flexible cord on your telephone, or invest in a cordless phone.
- Set up ground rules for when you're on the phone. You might tell your child, "Call me if you need help in the bathroom. Otherwise, unless it's an emergency, I want you to play quietly when I'm on the phone." This lets your child know your expectations.
- Have a variety of toys or games which your child can use independently. Then place these in a cabinet, closet, or box and label it, "telephone toys." Your child may only use those items when you're on the phone. Rotate the items periodically, and be consistent: "When I hang up the phone, you put away the toys."
- Be realistic. If it's supper time and your child is in the high chair, take a message and return the phone call later.

A pro-active posture is most important when a child is young. As a child grows up, the child will naturally adopt some of the preventative patterns you have modeled.

5   ✖ Apply Appropriate Child Management Techniques

There is no single, correct way to respond in a problem situation. The timing, consequences, circumstances, and people involved are just a few of the elements that make each episode unique.

However, here are some guidelines to serve as reference points when these situations arise:

Be Consistent If your child isn't allowed to do something, giving in "just this once" will make it more difficult to apply a rule next time. If you want to change a rule, change it, but be consistent.

Communicate Consequences Make sure your child understands that behavior has consequences. Avoid statements such as "You need to take out the garbage or else. . . ." Instead, say, "If you lie to me again about going to the mall, you will lose phone privileges for a week. That means you cannot receive or make any calls. Do you understand?"

Be Specific with Directions To a parent, "Clean up the bathroom" might mean scour the sink, clean off the counter, wipe out the shower, mop the floor, and replace the towels. To a child, "Clean the bathroom" might mean he should pick up the sock he left near the tub.

In this example, the parent and child perceived something different, yet both were right from their point of view. Make sure your child understands what you want before you punish him for not meeting your expectations.

Encourage Independent Problem-Solving Many, many discipline situations could be prevented if the parent would stay out of peer and sibling situations. Encourage your child to discuss the problem with the person involved and work toward a solution without calling you for help.

Act Quickly If action is needed, apply it directly after the incident. If your child takes a dollar today from the kitchen drawer to buy a piece of candy, show him immediately that this was wrong.

Avoid Arguing A discussion can result in positive action; an argument always involves winning, losing, and elements of control. It takes two to argue, so just walk away from your child if necessary.

Set Only Needed Rules Try to develop cooperative guidelines, set by you and your child. There's no benefit in testing the statement, "A rule is made to be broken."

Support Self-discipline A teen has the inner controls needed to monitor his own actions; a toddler doesn't. But the parent who stops the toddler from trying to pull the electric cord out of the wall is helping the child learn what is wrong and what is right. Set clear limits for behavior, then support your child as he develops inner controls to distinguish what is right and what is wrong.

6 ✺ Love Yourself; Love Your Child

Psychologists tell us that before you can truly help others feel good about themselves, you must feel good about yourself. With God's help, we can overcome our sinful nature. With God's help, we can change what we don't like. And on that basis, we can move forward to like ourselves, and love a child completely and unconditionally.

Say It Children are never too old to hear, "I love you." Where and how we say those words, though, changes through the years:

- We say, "I love you" with a hug and kiss, as a child walks through the kindergarten door.
- We say, "I love you" with a squeeze around the shoulders as a daughter turns sweet sixteen.
- We say, "I love you" with sadness, joy, and pride as a son takes the arm of his bride before the altar.

Show It A parent shows love in many ways: scrimping to save money for that cheerleading uniform or listening to endless hours of the squeaky violin rendition of "Twinkle, twinkle, little star."

Write It But we also need to write the words, "I love you" in lunchbox notes, sign postcards on a business trip, and date birthday cards.

List here the ways you will communicate to your child, "I love you," today:

1. _____

2. _____

3. _____

7 ❧ Turn Transitions into Launching Points

Parents often define transitions as "those awkward moments." When you pull into the driveway after a long trip and everybody wants to pet the cat, play in the sandbox, and do anything but unpack the car. Or that time between the end of the afternoon cartoon and serving supper. Those are typical transitions.

But you can change those lost (at best) or negative (at worst) transitions into valuable launching points for your family.

Timing is important, so be alert for possibilities to:

Continue a Good Thing If you've had family devotions during the days before Christmas, continue that same pattern even after the holiday decorations are put away.

Or, if you've spent a couple extra minutes talking around the dinner table one evening, say, "I liked this time together. Let's do this every night this week." Even if you only spend an extra moment or two, you're continuing something that can have a positive impact on your family.

Start a New Pattern If the dentist suggests your child spend more time brushing her teeth, make a tooth brushing chart to hang on the refrigerator immediately after you return from the appointment. Or, if your child is leaving school papers all over the living room, start a new pattern the first day of school after a vacation. Simply label a specific place (on a counter, dresser, table, etc.) "Johnny's school papers." Talk with your child before he leaves for school, and positively reinforce your child's new pattern after school.

End Something Negative If your child has had a problem with making her bed daily, jointly set a time when the pattern will stop. You might choose the beginning of a new week, a new month, or the day after her birthday.

8 🦋 Program Car Pools for Success

Car pooling offers these advantages:

- Helps a parent practice good time management.
- Offers built-in support system for parent.
- Provides a social opportunity for a child.
- Provides the parent with an opportunity to observe his child in a social situation.
- Reduces the "hassle factor" of a busy schedule.

Before ride-sharing begins, set some ground rules that every parent will agree to follow. Rules do not need to be in writing, but a car pool can be programmed for success when all drivers discuss basic points in advance.

Car Safety Rules

- Everyone must buckle the seat belt before the car starts.
- Riders in third grade and above may open and close car doors.

- Children leave the car by the door that's next to the curb. This eliminates children getting out of a car in the middle of the street.

- After dropping off a child, the driver waits at a house until an adult comes to the door. An unlocked door does not necessarily mean someone is home to care for a child.

- No food, drinks, or gum chewing is allowed in a car.

Contingency Plans During the set-up process, determine an alternate procedure to follow when children, parents, or cars are sick. If the car pool will transport children with gear (school bags, tennis rackets, pompons, wet swimsuits, and towels, etc.) agree on some basic guidelines. (For example, a child should change from a wet swimsuit before coming into the car, or all tennis rackets go in the trunk.)

Time and Place Also set up a specific time block for picking up and returning a child. ("I'll come between 12:50 and 1 P.M.") This gives each parent a margin of time if a baby needs a fast diaper change or a child needs a quick drink of water.

Determine an exact pick-up place. This is essential when large numbers of people will be leaving at the same time.

9 🦋 Make the Most of Car Time

Parents and children invest a significant amount of time riding together in a car. But you can maximize time spent in the car. The result will be safer driving, a happier child, and the opportunity to invest in the parent-child relationship.

Here is a blueprint for valuable car time:

Provide Something to Do Review the following materials frequently to ensure they are age appropriate for your child and other riders. Playthings can be stored in a cloth carrier which hangs over a seat or packaged individually in a box stored underneath or next to a seat. Set aside a regular time (for example, after church each week) to rotate these items:

- cassette tape/book sets with headphones. Package each set individually in a clear, self-sealing bag (check cassette batteries periodically).

- books. Store in a cardboard box between the seats or on the car floor; select books with short bites of information—joke books, atlas, picture dictionary, science encyclopedia, pop up, and variety books, etc.

- hand-held games.
- writing materials. Store in a box with a sturdy lid that can serve as a drawing table; include washable crayons and various kinds of paper.
- items that require no adult supervision, such as origami (paper folding) book and paper; "grab bag" of items from fast food children's meal packs; poseable figures; small construction set.

Talk and Listen Horns might toot, but the phone won't ring and an older sibling won't be listening around the corner to what you and your child discuss.

Enjoy Music Tune into the local Christian radio station. Sing along with the music and your child. Or pop a cassette into the tape deck. Take turns selecting tapes for listening.

10 ✖ Encourage Self-reliant Behavior

Can your child do it? If so, don't *you* do it. This is the basic way to encourage independence. The suggestions below will help you with the physical actions that propel a child toward independence.

Develop a Sense of Confidence Help your child develop a sense of confidence when approaching new tasks. Before a child will be open to learning, he must believe in himself as a child of God who has been blessed with talents and gifts. Sometimes this means you must review personal strengths and abilities with a child.

For example, if your preteen is riding a bus alone for the first time, you might tick off all the things that have prepared her for this event: riding a bus with you, having correct change, knowing how to pull the bell cord, and knowing what stop comes before her stop. Then the praise you offer consistently, specifically, and honestly will help your child begin such new efforts with a sense of confidence.

Give Your Child a Chance Your child is continuing to develop new capabilities, better judgment, and increased skills that can be adapted and applied in a variety of settings. Think back to what your child could do just one year ago in choosing his wardrobe. How has he grown? How could you encourage more self-reliant actions in this single area?

Have Realistic Expectations A child will not make a bed perfectly the first time. He will need assistance, time, and your patient understanding before the bed looks neat. Adjust your expectations to fit your child.

Value Learning It's a bonus when rewards can be built into a task. A child who clips food coupons from the newspaper and organizes them might earn a percentage of the money saved.

Build on Interests Periodically, ask your child, "What would you like to learn about cooking, washing windows, or the garage?" You might be surprised! But this offers a wonderful opportunity to build on your child's own interests.

Focus on Specifics As you identify new opportunities for independence, focus on a specific task. Identify what your child can do now, then look ahead to what he'll be ready to attempt at the next stage. This allows your child to build new skills onto what he already knows.

For example:

- Three-year-old: put napkins on the dinner table
- Four-year-old: set out silverware
- Five-year-old: set plates and cups
- Six-year-old: wipe off the table
- Seven-year-old: put away silverware

Evaluate Growth Consider your personal comfort level as your child adds new areas of responsibility. You might not want a child to run a vacuum cleaner until two years after your neighbor lets his child do that. Follow your own timeline, but continually increase your child's responsibilities.

11 ❡ Maximize Your Time

Each parent has the same number of minutes in the day. The challenge is to use time effectively.

Use a Calendar Write everything (even little things you're sure to remember!) on a family-sized calendar: the day you drive car pool, take snacks to preschool, or need to send money for a new lunch ticket.

Locate your calendar:

- where everyone can see it easily.
- in a place it will always stay.
- by the phone used most often.
- with a pencil attached. (Tie a pencil onto a string.)
- near a pack of Post-it notes.

Prioritize You might divide tasks for a single day into what must be done, what would be nice to do, and extras. Make a written list so you can check off the items when completed.

Create a Routine Begin with set events: mealtimes, going to the babysitter, bedtime. Then plan specific routines around those key points of the day. For example, at bedtime a child might put on pajamas, brush teeth, choose a book (or two or three) to read with you, say prayers, get up for water and the bathroom, say good night to the dog, and go to bed.

Other time blocks can be organized throughout the day in similar ways, but don't over-organize. Create routines that work.

Explain Time Management Help your child practice good time management techniques. Although the focus is on the child, children's routines can impact the entire family schedule. Sometimes a child's routine must be changed, adapted, or dropped when it's no longer positive or productive. Here's an example:

> "Julie, if you don't practice your lesson more often you're going to have to stop piano," said her mother.
>
> "Now that cheerleading has started, I don't have time to practice after school. But I really want to take piano, at least until after the spring recital," said Julie.
>
> "What are the options?" her mother asked.
>
> "I could stop cheerleading, but I'd never do that," said Julie quickly.

> "Or you could get up fifteen minutes earlier during the week and practice a couple more times on the weekends," said her mother.
>
> "I guess so," said Julie. "Or I could have a lesson every other week."

In this situation, the mother helped her daughter learn how to prioritize, reorganize blocks of time, make decisions about the use of time, and still achieve her goals.

Be Flexible Count on interruptions: they are a part of any parent's day. If they don't happen, enjoy your extra moments!

Forget the Small Stuff Don't invest time and energy on little decisions. Thoughtful decision-making requires time and emotional energy. So if your child wants to use the phone in the bedroom instead of the kitchen, or if your child wants to watch television from 4 to 4:30 instead of 4:30 to 5, that's fine. Invest time in big decisions that count, such as, "Which preschool is the best match for my child and the family?" or "Will adding trombone lessons be too much for my child, work into the budget, and fit into the schedule?"

List Quickie Tasks Post a list of kitchen "quickies" on the refrigerator. The average adult spends two years playing telephone tag, so include jobs that can be done quietly while on the phone or waiting for bread to finish baking: wipe the counter, scour the sink, clean a shelf, wipe fingerprints off woodwork, etc.

Capture Quality Moments Fill a kitchen drawer or cabinet with parent-child "quickies." Include games that can be played in five minutes or less (card games, paper and pencil for tic-tac-toe, etc.) and books that can be read quickly. Rotate items periodically, so you and your child always have the potential to capture quality moments.

12 ✖ Tame the Schedule

There is a seemingly endless number of children's organized activities.

How much is too much? Ask yourself: Does my child see more of the back of my head (as you're driving) than my face? Then follow these five steps before committing your child to any activity:

Measure the Time Total the amount of time the activity will require. Record the actual class or activity time, travel time and extras, driving other children home if you car pool, for example.

Consider Costs List basic expenses. Then ask specific questions about hidden costs: recitals, meets, tournaments, uniform, shoes, extra lessons, bus, required insurance, and equipment.

Consult Your Calendar Add information about this potential activity to your master calendar.

Assess the Situation Ask: What would this new activity change? How would it affect the family as a unit?

Make Choices The activity tolerance level changes with the season, the parent, the child, and specific demands of the particular activity. You or your children might need to select from many good activities. Base your decision on what is best for your family, not what works for your neighbor.

Remember: When you consider children's activities, more isn't necessarily better for you or your child.

13 ✳ Get That Feeling

Right now, how do you feel? If you're tired from getting up during the night with a sick child, or happy that your child made a goal in the soccer game, how you feel will even influence your reading of this book.

Your emotional tone also influences how your child's day will go. If you wake up grumpy and stay grumpy all day, your child probably won't have a great day, either.

Identify the Atmosphere Make a conscious effort to establish a positive atmosphere. One parent might want a feeling of caring, concern for each other, and cooperation. Another parent might seek a sense of peace to surround her children. But what qualities are important for the emotional tone that surrounds your child? Identify what you want.

Establish the Environment Now you can focus on the elements that contribute to "that feeling." For example, if you want a loving atmosphere, you will need to model, reinforce, give, and receive love. If you want a peaceful tone, everyone will avoid yelling at the dog, calling from the basement to the attic, and turning on the television.

Know the Crunch Point As you examine the atmosphere, identify times of the day when your terrific feeling disintegrates. Typical crunch points for parents include before a child leaves for school in the morning, before supper, and right at bedtime.

Adapt Your Situation Once you've identified the tough time frames, think through exactly what must get done during those segments. Consider what tasks can be moved to less crowded times of the day, decide if some activities can be done by others who are less hassled, and look at ways you can simplify the "must do" jobs.

Then ask: Are my expectations realistic? If not, expand the time frame or go back to thinking!

14 ✹ Invest in Safety

"The physical safety of my child" consistently ranks in the top five concerns for parents. Major danger areas for children include the car, bicycles, and water. Protecting and preventing problems in these areas requires time, thought, and money, but there's no question about the value of the investment.

Buckle up The familiar words, "Buckle up" really shouldn't be necessary. But recent statistics showed that just over half of parents surveyed correctly used their child's car seat. Avoid a problem: Look at the pictures and read the directions that are packaged with your child's seat. Check periodically that your child still fits the guidelines for the particular system you're using. After all, a child will complain that "My shoes are too tight" when he needs a new pair of shoes, but few children will say, "I need a different car seat."

When you shop for a car seat, buy a new one. This is one time when it won't pay to shop garage sales and resale shops. Restraint system regulations change frequently; recalls happen all too often.   Register the car seat directly with the company, so you can be contacted in case of a problem.

If buckling up is still a problem in your car, say, "This car will move only when everyone's strapped in." If someone tries to unbuckle while you're driving, pull over to the side of the road, stop the car, get out and solve the problem, and don't move until everyone is buckled up again.

Be Careful Around Water Avoid the silent accidents.   Statistics show the typical drowning victim is a "boy between the age of 1 and 3 who is not thought to be in the pool or spa area." There is an increasing number of home Jacuzzis, spas, and pools. If you or a neighbor have any container deeper than a birdbath that is filled with water, be extra alert.

Remember that young children develop new skills and abilities each day.   If your child can't open a sliding door today, he might be able to do that tomorrow.   If she can't pull open the hot tub lid today, she might be able to do it tomorrow. Invest in swimming lessons as soon as possible, but just because your child can swim, don't reduce your watchfulness.

Use Helmets Hang a helmet on the handlebars.   Give your child a helmet along with her first bike.   State the rule clearly: Every single time you climb on the bike, you must wear the helmet. Then show her how to adjust the helmet to fit safely. Younger children, especially, tend to pull the helmet down over their ears, exposing the vulnerable front part of their head. Follow directions exactly for the helmet you purchased; helmets adjust in various ways and one helmet when worn properly can feel slightly different from another helmet. If you or other family members ride with your child, wear a helmet; parent safety counts too!

If your child balks at wearing a helmet, the complaints will most likely be one of the following:

- *"Nobody else wears one."* Involve your school in sponsoring a bike clinic, perhaps with the local police department.
- *"A helmet is hot."* Professional football players would agree. But temperature doesn't change the important protection a helmet can give.
- *"A helmet is a bother."* Yes, it is, especially if you ride to school and it won't fit in a locker.

15 ✖ Practice the "S" Word

What does a new parent crave more than anything else? You're right: the "s" word.

Use these suggestions for sweet days and sweet dreams:

Follow a Nighttime Routine Set up a regular pattern of activities so the children know what comes next. After we say good night to the gerbils, we need to brush our teeth. After we brush teeth, we need to lay out clothes for tomorrow. A routine can help a child stay focused.

Make a Bedtime Schedule Begin with the desired time for "lights out." Then back up your schedule to include every possible distraction. Allow for the inevitable stalls (kissing the teddy bear, running back to the bathroom, etc.) Use this as a guideline.

Make Bedtime a Good Time Share a devotion. Pray for loved ones. Ask your child to recall the events of the day. Talk about tomorrow. Sing a song. Tell your child, "I love you." Give your child a hug or kiss. Sit next to her bed. Make this a time to be emotionally and physically close to your child.

Clarify the Consequences of Stalling
Communicate very clearly what will happen if your child gets up fifteen times before falling asleep. For example: "If you get up again, I will take out the nightlight" or "If you get up another time, your door will be closed." This will reduce the number of frustrating interruptions in your evening and help your child get to sleep in a peaceful manner.

Support Bedtime Keep the house quieter after your child is in bed. Lower the volume of the television. Close the door if you talk on the phone. A child often stays awake because he feels he might miss something. If something exciting *is* going on, keep it quiet.

Sleep Whenever and Wherever You Can
If the baby is asleep, go to bed, even if it's not your bedtime. If you're on the sidelines of a baseball game, and your child's not up to bat in this inning, close your eyes. Rest at every opportunity. Medical personnel say most people can't get too much sleep. And many parents agree with that!

16 ✖ Practice Wellness

Wellness isn't something you put on like boots or buy like a head of lettuce. Wellness is a way of life.

Exercise Build physical activity into the family routine. You might swim with your child at the YMCA, walk around the block with the dog every night after supper, but do something regularly.

Let your child try a variety of sports and activities. Pay for a single series of roller skating, judo, or ballet lessons, just to give your child the experience. Often, a child doesn't exercise because he hasn't discovered an activity she enjoys.

Don't Rush It's easy to add the words, "Hurry up" when a parent talks to a child. But only give that direction if absolutely necessary. Each person develops a personal pace. Too much hurrying isn't good for you or your child.

Be Health Conscious Communicate to your child that wellness is normal. Teach your child that being active isn't just for athletes, reading labels isn't only for health food nuts, and caring about pollution caused by the lawn mower isn't just for activists.

Stop the inter-generational cycle of bad habits with this generation. Identify the automatic responses that aren't good. Catch yourself when it seems cheaper to throw away a bottle than recycle it, or salt the meatloaf simply because your mother always did. If you want some help and support, ask your child to stop you! That will make her more aware and contribute to more responsive family living.

Have Regular Checkups   Keep immunizations up-to-date. And each time you submit a medical form to school, keep a copy for your personal files.

The best time to prepare your child for a visit to a dentist or medical doctor is when she's healthy. This is a good time to encourage her to share feelings and concerns without the added stress that comes with illness or injury.

Don't Procrastinate   Benjamin Franklin's old adage, "Never put off until tomorrow what you can do today," was quite correct: procrastination increases stress. What do you want to accomplish today? Make a list, keep it realistic, and then do it.

17 ❧ Go It Alone

Ideally, a parent should look for opportunities to build three kinds of alone time into the family schedule:

- time alone for the parent
- time alone for the child
- time alone for the parent with each child

Unfortunately, no parent lives in an ideal world with unlimited time. So it's up to you to claim and plan for these kinds of alone time whenever possible.

Time alone for a parent is so important it relates to an entirely separate issue in this book. (See the next chapter "Take a Break" for details.) But the other "alone times" are equally important.

One-on-One Time Each child needs to feel important to you. One way to communicate this is to focus specifically on that child. You might spend five minutes a day reading to him, ten minutes at bedtime, or a half hour together after supper. The amount of time is not the most important factor (although generally, the more time, the better). What counts is that your focus is the individual child and your relationship.

You benefit from this one-on-one time by:

- maintaining a sense of where your child is and where he is going.

- knowing what is important to him, his fears and concerns, his joys and what makes him smile.

- ensuring continuing communication.

A Child's Alone Time As soon as your child is old enough to be alone safely, she needs real alone time too. This isn't "time out" for inappropriate behavior or a cooling off period for use of bad language. Alone time offers the opportunity to play, think, pray, and daydream.

Alone time has become more important because of the dramatic increase in the number of organized activities for children. With so many opportunities for social interaction, many children today know how to share and play. But many of these same children need to learn how to live with themselves. Alone time begins with the two-and-one-half-year-old, who reads books in her room before settling down for a nap. A five-year-old's version of alone time might be those moments after waking up, when she plays quietly with toys until others in the family are awake.

A teen's version of alone time might be spent paging through old school yearbooks or a box of letters, a time to relax before starting homework after school.

Alone time might be five minutes or an hour. The guidelines will change as your child grows up. But when your child returns to the family from alone time, you'll be happy to see him and he'll come with revived emotional energy.

Home Alone Please note: Alone time is very different from being home alone. At what age a child is left home alone depends on a variety of factors, including age and personality of the child, how long the child will be alone, how far away a parent will be, whether or not younger siblings are also home, if the time includes daylight or nighttime hours, if the child comes home alone to an empty house, knowledge of emergency procedures, etc.

Alone time, as described in this chapter, implies the parent or other adult is home. Being home alone is one of the issues you and your child will face in helping him build a sense of responsibility.

18 ❊ Take a Break

Sip a glass of water.
Close your eyes.
Lean your head back.
Stretch. Yawn.
It feels good to take a break, doesn't it?

With so much variety in the life of a parent, some people might wonder how parenting can ever get boring. Yet veterans would respond, "It doesn't get boring. Parents just need a break from all the excitement!"

Every parent benefits from a change of these three elements in a typical day with a child:

- place
- pace
- people

Go Someplace Consider these five places:

- Window shop.
- Visit an older person.
- Go to the library.
- Walk around the block.

- Visit a museum in the off-season.

Change Your Pace Consider these five paces:

- Browse through a catalog.
- Set the kitchen timer for five minutes. Do something that will make you feel good.
- Read a book or chapter of a book from your child's bookshelf.
- Learn a new craft or skill.
- Bake a cake for someone "just because."

Consider People Consider these five people:

- Look through a family picture or scrapbook.
- Write to a relative.
- Phone a friend.
- Look in the mirror.
- Write a note to someone you love (maybe even your child!).

19 🦋 Cope Realistically with Sibling Rivalry

Rivalry is part of a sibling relationship. The jockeying for position and a parent's love, time, and affection, however, can skew a parent's focus. Sibling relationships become even more complicated in the case of blended family groupings.

The most competitive siblings tend to be those close in age and of the same sex. An older child fears a younger one will catch up; a younger one is challenged to do just that. Regardless of family size or shape, every child needs to see that he has a special place of value. Every child must know, "I am important in this family." Comparisons between children happen naturally; but a parent must be sensitive to how this single action, especially when done repeatedly, can fuel sibling rivalry. Look at this example:

> Jason keeps his room messy.
> Whitney keeps her room neat.

Both children know you will check their room on Saturday morning. After looking at both children's rooms, here is how two different parents handle the same situation:

Parent One: "Jason, I want you to come into Whitney's room and see how neat it is."

Jason stomps into Whitney's room, muttering under his breath. He takes a brief look at his sister's "perfect" room, stomps back to his bedroom where he grabs a baseball card and one dirty sock off the floor and throws them into the closet. Then he plops back on the bed.

Parent Two: "Whitney, your room is so neat. Even the books look great stacked nicely on the shelf." Parent Two then goes to Jason's room and says, "Jason, your bedcovers are so straight today. That's great. Can you find three things I might trip on if I walked to the window? Please move them."
Jason sighs, tosses the items into the closet, and plops back on the bed.

The end result is the same: Jason ends up on his bed and his bedroom floor is marginally cleaner. But Parent Two handled each child individually and did not fuel rivalry between the two children.

Use these additional suggestions to cope with sibling rivalry:

Teach Sensitivity Other people's feelings matter. A common example is name-calling. A parent might prohibit this behavior in the backyard with friends, but almost ignore it completely when name-calling is directed at siblings. A parent must intervene in such situations.

Acknowledge Contributions Take every opportunity to emphasize a child's individual contribution to the family. For example, when you kiss your child good-night at bedtime, recall one way in which he added something positive to the day. You might say, "Thanks for answering the phone when I was taking the muffins from the oven," or "I appreciated your help folding the clothes today."

Develop Competence One child might enjoy playing soccer; another might enjoy becoming a trombonist. Explore a wide range of options for each child, so that even a child with physical limitations or learning problems can find an area of competence. Excelling at something gives a child enjoyment and a sense of accomplishment, but it also gives others an opportunity to applaud his efforts.

Monitor Yourself Watch your own words and actions. It's easy to fall into a pattern of building up one child while putting down another.

20 Come, Summer

"Summertime, and the living is easy" offers an incorrect description of June, July, and August for many parents. Yet the summer months offer a change of routine, outdoor activity options, and a chance to regroup.

Have Unscheduled Time Allow your child some unscheduled time. A child might need extra sleep and more "nothingness" to cope with the end of one experience and the beginning of a new experience. Change requires some getting-used-to time.

Take It Easy Ease into your summer schedule. Make sure your child knows in advance the procedure for hanging up the swimsuit, putting away the bike, and the rules for leaving the yard to play at a friend's house.

Set Goals Decide what you want for your child. Don't list specific programs; instead, focus on goals. For example, do you want him to:

- learn skills that will help him in school? Talk with your child's teacher. Get specific suggestions regarding his needs and areas for improvement.

- get enrichment he wouldn't get in school? If so, request the summer schedule from area museums and agencies.

- develop relationships with family members? Contact relatives in advance; summer schedules fill up quickly.

- become more independent? Your child might attend a camp away from home or learn to manage his time more effectively at home.

During the summer months, evaluate your plans and make needed adjustments.

Support Learning When possible, take your child on errands and trips to local historic sites. Go with him regularly to the library. Watch the evening news together, or read the newspaper together. Look especially for summer-only opportunities: the county fair, circus, berry-picking, church programs, etc.

Plan Christmas Begin your list of Christmas presents. Check out idea books from the air-conditioned library, and spend hot summer evenings in a cool basement, working on Christmas projects. This can be a very refreshing change of pace, and will be a real head start toward enjoying the holidays.

Think Safety Be alert to seasonal safety hazards.

- At the beach, apply sunscreen to the tops of feet, noses, tops of shoulders, and other areas that aren't normally exposed to the sun. Remember to cover your child's head, especially if you have a young one; infants and toddlers might not have thick hair that can help protect their scalp.

- The barbecue grill can appear deceptively friendly to a young child. Make sure your child knows the grill and utensils are off-limits.

- Sand, pavement, and asphalt can get burning hot under the summer sun. Set and enforce a shoe policy.

Avoid Overscheduling A child needs some free time during every season of the year. Don't overbook the summer months.

Earn Money Host a garage sale. Go through closets and toy shelves. Let your child host a lemonade stand or help a neighbor weed her garden.

21 ✖ Know Yourself

You are the key to valuable information which can dramatically influence your parenting. You bring unique strengths, background experiences, and perceptions to parenting. You know yourself, your situation, and your child better than anyone else. You have a lot to offer your child. Stay on the cutting edge of parenting by keeping in touch with yourself. Use the following guidelines to help you:

Know Your "Pace" Apply to your parenting what you know about your personal pace. Are you a morning person? If so, use the morning hours to work through the questions about whether or not Johnny can play on the tennis team. Do you feel wiped out after supper? Then postpone that discussion of Johnny and the tennis team to another time. Do you feel grumpy on a rainy day? Invigorated after a snowstorm? Wisely apply knowledge about your personal rhythms and mood swings.

Accept Certain Facts

- Being a parent will always be a part of who I am.
- Being a parent has changed me.

These statements are true whether you have an infant or teenager, are employed or stay at home, single or married, young or old, have a house full of young children or live across the country from a grandchild. Don't try to take the "parent" out of your personhood. Even if your child is grown, you will probably always be concerned about his well-being. You will always be a parent.

Recognize Your Needs You have certain needs as a parent. Would you be a more effective parent right now if you had a reliable support system? Do you need more sleep? More breaks from your child? Fill in the blanks below:

- Something I need now that will help me be a better parent:

  _____

- One way I can meet this need:

  _____

- One probable way my parenting will benefit:

  _____

22 ❧ Avoid Homework Hassles

Homework is assigned to reinforce or practice new skills, help a child build positive study habits and good time management techniques, or extend, expand, or enhance classroom learning. Homework is part of a child's school experience, but it can easily become a source of conflict between parent and child.

Avoid the homework hassle with these guidelines:

Establish a Study Place Provide a quiet, well-lit place for your child to work. Reduce distractions, so a child won't be tempted to half-listen to a television or stereo. Your child will need pencils, paper, a place to spread out books and papers, and possibly some study aids including an atlas, dictionary, etc.

Set Study Rules Set rules that meet your child's specific needs. Examples include these two: No television until homework is done. You may only call friends after homework is done or to check homework with them.

Help Constructively Support your child, but don't deprive him of the chance to learn by doing his assignment. If he asks for your help:

- Suggest he take a break. A drink of water or time to stretch won't physically give him a clearer head, but it can provide just a slight change of pace so he can return to the work somewhat refreshed.

- Ask him for background information on the topic to find out what he already knows. Just thinking through and then verbally reviewing prior knowledge can help a child pull things together in his own mind.

- Ask him to read the directions aloud to you. You might be able to phrase the directions more clearly.

- Review the directions with him to make sure he understands the assignment. Sometimes another interpretation is helpful.

- Encourage him to review the textbook (including glossary, charts, maps, graphs) or class notes for additional information.

- Let your child teach *you.* This is one of the best ways for him to understand the material.

- Ask questions about the material that will lead him to understand or complete the assignment.
- As a last resort, suggest he phone a classmate or local homework hotline for assistance.

Consult the Teacher If your child consistently has so much homework he doesn't have time to unwind, you might speak with the teacher or school administrator. The teacher might not realize how much time certain kinds of assignments actually take. Your feedback can be very helpful when presented in a nonthreatening manner. Find out from other parents if their children are having similar homework struggles. If your child is alone, the problem might not be the amount of homework, but time management or work study skills. If classmates are having similar problems, join with other parents and talk with the administrator. In this situation, there is strength in numbers.

Also consult the teacher if your child appears to have consistent problems in one subject area or with one particular kind of question or type of problem. Find out if your child has similar difficulties at school. By working together, you and the teacher might discover something about your child that can dramatically affect his performance. Here are some real examples from classroom teachers:

- "I didn't know until I talked with Mrs.____ that Jessica's father had left the state and the family is having terrible financial trouble."
- "Mr. _____told me that Tyler doesn't hear well out of one ear, but that information wasn't recorded on his records. I would have never known that if Mr. _____ hadn't complained about Tyler's low grades last quarter."
- "Tracy's grandfather died a couple weeks ago. When I talked with her mother about the sudden slide in her grades, she told me that might be the reason. Tracy was very close to her grandfather. I wish Mrs.____ had told me sooner."

Volunteer Volunteer to take your child to the library, buy an assignment notebook, or help with other special needs. These important opportunities show you support his school work.

23 Participate at School

Your participation is important: researchers consistently conclude that children perform better in school when their parents are involved. This is true for children of all ages, in all situations, at all levels through high school. Make school participation one of your highest priorities. Before the year begins, consider ways in which you can be involved.

Identify Your Role Answer these questions to help you identify a school role:

- What time segments will you have available?
- What talents can you share?
- Would you like to work with others or alone?
- Do you want to help your child's teacher or would you be willing to assist with any school project?
- In what ways could you contribute the most as a school volunteer?

Think through these issues, but be flexible so you can honestly accept the way in which the school can best put your talents to use.

Attend School Functions Whenever possible accept the invitation to attend school functions: open house, parent-teacher conference, parent-teacher meeting. Also consider other opportunities to eat lunch with your child in the school cafeteria, lead playground games, talk to your child's class about your job, or give a presentation about a place you've visited. These activities state very clearly, "I care about my child's school life."

Don't Insist on Your Own Way Avoid some of the pitfalls that sometimes accompany parent involvement. For example:

- *I want to volunteer in specific ways.* Be upfront and honest, right from the beginning. If you have certain terms ("I want to cook with the kindergarten class the first Friday of every month") be aware that your volunteering might not match up with school needs.
- *My child should get preferential treatment* (lead in the school play, first-string on the baseball team, etc.) *because I'm so active at school.* Your motivation should be to demonstrate support for your child and make your school a better place for your child and other children. Although you might become personally acquainted with staff members, it's improper to expect

your child to be treated differently than
any other child.

- *I should be thanked for my participation.*
  Unfortunately, that doesn't always happen. Volunteers should be honored at a
  school breakfast, recognized at an assem-
  bly, or given special nametags to wear.
  Schools don't always take the time or
  make the effort to do that. Get satisfaction
  from knowing that you've contributed to
  your child's education, and then any ac-
  colades will simply be nice extras.

- *The teacher should support my child when
  there's a disagreement because the
  teacher knows I care so much.* One of the
  most common mistakes a parent can
  make is to communicate to school personnel, "My child's perfect. My child wouldn't
  start a fight, spray water from the fountain, throw food in the cafeteria, etc."

- *I should be thanked for my participation.*
  Unfortunately, that doesn't always happen. Volunteers should be honored at a
  school breakfast, recognized at an assem-
  bly, or given special nametags to wear.
  Schools don't always take the time or
  make the effort to do that. Get satisfaction
  from knowing that you've contributed to
  your child's education, and then any ac-
  colades will simply be nice extras.

24 ✖ Offer Choices

So much in a child's life is totally beyond his control. A parent must make many decisions: an infant can't decide what food is best; a toddler doesn't know that holding your hand tightly is one of the safest ways to cross a street; a preteen girl might not comprehend how buying (and wearing) a skimpy dress can give an inappropriate message to a thirteen-year-old boy.

But as a child grows up, it's developmentally appropriate for a parent to back off from making all the decisions. A child should gradually learn how to choose between alternatives. Making choices gives a child a greater sense of control. A child who has made choices throughout life will approach major decisions with a greater awareness of options and an ability to live with choices.

Begin Simply Begin with simple choices that relate to concrete items. For example, say "Do you want to read the book about the teddy bear or the choo-choo train?"

When you offer choices, be sure you can live with whatever your child chooses. In the example above, if you don't want your child to pick the bear book, change the offer to include two alternatives which you would accept willingly. For example, "Do you want to read about the choo-choo train or the truck?"

Some children can stubbornly refuse to accept any of the choices offered. If you feel your child might willingly accept either choice on another day, simply restate the options with one addition:

> "Your choice is having me read about the choo-choo train, the truck, or we don't have to read at all."

In addition, give your child the opportunity to make many nonverbal choices. Offer both thick and thin crayons; keep short, long, thick and thin pencils on his desk; write a list of chores that need to be done by the end of the day, but they can be done at any time and in any order. Your child will practice decision-making very naturally, and repeatedly, during normal activities.

Increase Complexity Gradually increase the number and complexity of choices. An older child should be able to decide when asked, "Do you want me to pick you up at the field after the game or would you rather go out with the team and take the bus back to school? You can phone me from there."

Offer actual choices. For example, there aren't any real options in this statement: "I can't talk on the phone if you're going to be noisy." Compare that to this statement which offers a choice: "I'm talking on the phone. You can play upstairs in your room or down in the basement. You choose."

Offering choices can also contribute directly to developing a willingness to cooperate in situations without options. For example, "Yesterday, when we went shopping, you had a choice of cereals. Today, since it's raining, you don't have a choice of taking or not taking an umbrella to school."

You will be able to choose many of the options from which your child can select when that child is young. But as he grows up, the options from which he will choose will be set by other people and circumstances beyond your area of control. This is a sign of normal growth and development.

25 Celebrate Traditions

The fabric of life is woven with routine. Routines that are repeated and tied to a specific time, person, or event can be called traditions. Family traditions join generations, celebrate life, remember death, and give a personal sense of order and purpose to life. People benefit so much from traditions that "celebrating traditions" is consistently noted by experts who study the qualities of strong families.

Changes in traditions have accompanied changes in the definition of family. This means that some activities—which have been anticipated, enjoyed, and remembered for years—won't continue in the current form. Family traditions change with time, place, and people.

How families get traditions has changed through the years. Generations have previously been linked directly through family rituals. Now, traditions are started by greeting card companies, sports schedules, the floral industry, and the media. (How many football games were watched on Thanksgiving Day at your house?) Be selective, so influences from outside the family have a positive effect on your own traditions.

Use these suggestions to strengthen your family through traditions:

Everyday Traditions The word "tradition" often is tied to holidays. But also consider building everyday traditions that help hold your family together. Conscious efforts to regularly do meaningful activities can strengthen your family unit. Go out to eat after church each week. Kiss each child before he leaves for school in the morning. Stay up late to talk to the teen who comes back after a date.

Appropriate Traditions Be sensitive to traditions that need to be changed. If buying Christmas presents for all the cousins puts an annual strain on the family budget, now is the time to change tradition. You might "draw" for the name of a single cousin for whom to purchase a gift. Or instead of exchanging gifts, each family unit can contribute to a favorite charity.

Make traditions fit your family. If Grandma has always hosted Christmas dinner but has recently moved into a small apartment, consider going out for dinner. If you want to use an Advent wreath in December but you're afraid of lighting candles with your young child around, keep the candles unlit. You can mold a tradition to meet your family needs.

Maintain Tradition Take responsibility for continuing traditions. If the recently-deceased Aunt Emma always organized an eagerly anticipated shower for a newborn, someone needs to fill Aunt Emma's place. Don't let good family practices die with the organizer. Families should use every opportunity to honor the elders, welcome the babies, and link the past, present, and future.

Acknowledge Changes People can legitimately state their disappointment, and in some ways, grieve the loss of meaningful traditions. Listen with sensitivity as your child asks, "Now that I have three Grandma's, is any Grandma coming for Thanksgiving?"

As people enter and leave your family circle, look for opportunities to establish new traditions. Ask the new members about their family rituals. Remember, you only need to do something once and you can have a new tradition!

26 ✹ Enjoy Christmas, Really!

Christmas comes with memories. No other holiday is so closely tied to family, tradition, and children. How a person views Christmas changes once that person becomes a parent. The hopes and dreams for a new generation get all wrapped up in Christmas. Here are some guidelines for a happy holiday:

Set Goals What do you and your child want from this holiday season? A child might answer that question with a long list of toys. But a parent comes to Christmas with other concerns. Perhaps you want to develop a closer relationship with a grandparent or reestablish ties with a friend. Maybe you want your child to focus on the real meaning of Christmas.

Think through the possibilities; then focus on what you actually want. Write that on the top of your December calendar. This will be a visual reminder of your goal.

Make This One Special Focus on the uniqueness of this particular Christmas. Consider:

- How can the music, decorations, and other "signs of the season" contribute to the unique emotional tone of your household this year?

- Developmentally, what can your child do this year that he couldn't do last Christmas?

- What family members and friends will be a part of your holidays this year?

- What particular format for sharing with friends (card, letter, personal note, etc.) fits your family this year?

- How will children's activities, travel plans, and work schedules influence your December schedule?

- What is an age-appropriate way for your children to share the Christmas gospel this year? For example, a three-year-old might sing a Sunday school song for grandparents; a nine-year-old might be able to read or recite the Christmas story from Luke 2 after Christmas dinner.

Create Memories What do you want your child to remember about Christmas? Identify just one or two traditions with long-term enjoyment potential. This can prevent older children from saying, "Christmas is just for little kids."

People of all ages like to see holiday decorations, go caroling, and deliver goodies to shut-in neighbors or the elderly. How children participate varies with their age, but these activities and others can be meaningful throughout the years.

Share Memories More than any other holiday, Christmas offers an opportunity to share your personal history with your child. Even a child who might automatically tune-out with the comment, "That's old time stuff," during another time of year might like to learn about Christmas in the "good old days." Use this opportunity to pass onto the next generation a favorite recipe, handicraft, or the history of a special tree ornament.

Go to Church Build church attendance into the Christmas Eve or Christmas Day schedule. If you have company for the holiday, invite them to join you. Even add a tradition onto the actual going to church: Take the family Christmas photos just before you leave for worship.

Celebrate the Season Focus on the entire Christmas season, not just on a single day. Spread out your activities over the entire month of December or beyond. Advent, which is a time of preparation for Christ's coming, is celebrated on the four Sundays before Christmas. Epiphany, or January 6, has been marked by many as the traditional end of the holiday season.

27 ❧ Answer Your Child's Questions

At one time or another, every parent is asked those questions most of us dread: "Mommy, my teacher said I came from a daddy seed. How did that work?" Or "Daddy, did you really run away from home like Grandma said?"

What can you say?

Be Honest "Be truthful" is good advice for Scouts and parents. Even very young children, who might not know how to read, know how to read emotions. If you lie or are evasive, you and God won't just share the secret: your child will know too. Avoid messy answers. Tell the truth the first time. For example:

- When a four-year-old shows you a masterpiece from preschool, avoid saying, "That's beautiful" when you're really thinking, "Is my daughter the only one who doesn't know how to hold a paintbrush?" Be honest, instead: "Oh, you used lots of orange. That's one of my favorite colors."

- When a teenager asks, "Mom, can I go shopping? Tracy and I are going to meet at 7," avoid saying, "I want you home tonight," unless that's really what you mean. A more honest response might be, "No, not tonight. Shopping at the mall once a week is enough."

And if you don't know the answer, be honest with this too:

- "I don't really know how the gas makes our car run."

Follow Your Child's Lead This will ensure your response really answers your child's question and is developmentally appropriate.

If a child asks, "Where did I come from?" the child might be looking for a simple answer such as, "You were born at Memorial Hospital." Begin with the simplest explanation, and then get feedback from your child with the question, "Is that what you wanted to know?"

Discover What He Knows Sometimes we need to find out what information our child already has, or check that facts are correct. If your preteen asks, "Can I go out with Greg?" don't panic. Ask, "What does going out mean?" The answer your child gives will guide your response. To a nine-year-old, "going out" might mean the two preadolescents never talk on the playground, just in the school hallway. To a twelve-year-old, "going out" might mean talking on the phone. To a sixteen-year-old, "going out" might mean sharing a pizza after a football game.

Postpone Questions When Necessary

Every parent has chuckled at cartoons that show a frazzled parent caught in a traffic jam while being asked a question about sex that requires a detailed answer. Unfortunately, this comical situation happens in real parenting.

If you get stuck like this, stall for the moment, but commit yourself to answer the question later. A good response is, "This isn't a good time, but I want to answer that. Let's talk about it after supper, tonight. That will give me a chance to think a little bit too."

Keep Communication Lines Open Show

by your words and nonverbal posture that you welcome your child's questions in the future. You might say, "Let me know if you ever have anything else like this you want to talk about."

28 ❦ Keep Talking

Good communication is a key element in healthy marriages, good family life, and even efficiently-run corporations. But "talking time" has decreased in families today.

Use these suggestions for effective communication:

Establish Eye Contact If you have a young child, that might mean kneeling down next to him. If you have a teenager, you might both sit at the kitchen table when you have a discussion.

Schedule Talking Time You might not need to write it on the family calendar, but then again, you might! Just make sure there is at least one time segment each day when the pace is intentionally relaxed to stimulate conversation. You might linger at the dinner table; you might all stay in the living room after turning off the evening news. Find a time that works for your family, and then stick around and listen.

Use Your Ears You'll learn more about your child if you listen. Ask for more information or share your viewpoint, but let your child lead the conversation.

Avoid Misunderstandings Miscommunication is almost inevitable when a parent calls to a child who's in another room or talks to a teen who's on the phone. Instead of saying, "Do you understand?" ask the child a question about the directions. For example, if you aren't sure a child heard you say, "Take the dog out for a walk before supper," followup with the question, "When will you walk the dog?"

Ask Productive Questions When you want to learn something, avoid questions that will result in a yes or no response. Don't ask, "Did you have fun at school today?" If you really want to know what happened during the day, ask, "With whom did you eat lunch today? What did you do in math? When did you laugh?"

Say "I love you" There are few things every parent must do every day, but this is one of them: say, "I love you," with feeling, to each child at least once a day. Also remember to show your child, "I love you" in many different ways.

Locate a Private Place Your child will talk with you more freely if he knows a sibling isn't hiding around the corner. When you need to talk privately with a child, go into a room and close the door. Or go to the car. Whether it's parked in your driveway or at a stoplight, a car can be an excellent place for personal sharing.

Don't Compete with Anything Your family will have better communication if you turn off the radio, electronic games, stereo, and television. Even background noise can be distracting during a conversation.

Avoid Repetition Repeat only words of love to a child. Avoid repeating directions for two reasons:

- When a child knows you'll say something only once, he'll learn to listen the first time.
- If a child knows you'll probably repeat something and then tunes you out, he might not tune you back in.

This single action of avoiding repetition will prevent an endless number of communication problems.

29 ❧ Pray

Prayer is talking and listening to God. A prayer relationship with God is the cornerstone of effective parenting.

Teach Your Child the Basics of Prayer

- To whom should you pray? We should only pray to God.

  ". . . 'You shall worship the LORD your God, and Him only you shall serve.'" (Matt. 4:10)

- What should you pray for? Anything that is needed. A parents' prayer can be as simple as "Please, Lord, give me patience until we sit down for supper," or a long statement from the heart.

  "Therefore do not worry, saying, 'What shall we eat?' or 'What shall we drink?' or 'What shall we wear?' For after all these things the Gentiles seek. For your heavenly Father knows that you need all these things." (Matt. 6:31–32)

- Will God answer my prayer? One of the challenges of parenting is to help a child understand that God answers prayer in His own time and in His own way: Not every child can have a puppy who asks God for one! But we can assure a child, just as we know in our hearts, that God will care for us, and provide what we need.

  > "Ask, and it will be given to you; seek, and you will find; knock, and it will be opened to you." (Matt. 7:7–8.)

- When can you pray? Anytime. A teen may pray before facing a final exam; a young child might talk to God at bedtime about an aging cat. God's prayer hotline is open to all children and parents, twenty-four hours a day.

  > "Pray without ceasing." (1 Thess. 5:17)

Pray Regularly Build prayer into your daily routine. You may offer a prayer before eating, at bedtime, or even before driving off on a family vacation. God will listen, whenever and wherever you pray.

Don't Worry about the "Gimmes" "God give me" is often the first way a child will pray. That simply reflects his developmental level since a young child views himself at the center

of the world. As he moves beyond that understanding, the "gimme" prayers become more
balanced with thanks and praise. (God accepts
"gimme" prayers from parents too!)

Respect Your Child's Prayers Sometimes children use the format of a spontaneous
prayer to communicate something to a parent.
This prayer from a four-year-old is an example:

> Dear God,
>   Please help my parents get me new boots.
> And please don't let it snow until I get my
> new boots. Amen.

A child can offer this kind of prayer with a
hidden agenda. He hopes you will overhear his
words and respond with the appropriate action.
Or a child can say such words from the heart
which he intends for God alone. Only God can
see into our child's heart; refrain from judging
what your child says and controlling what form
your child uses for prayer.

Give It Time A child can learn the words,
"God has infinite wisdom" but many young ones
simply say, "God is smart." Even knowing that,
like some adults, your child might try to "help
God" by suggesting what He should do. Remember that truly learning to let God lead in life
might take a long time.

30 ❦ Provide Christian Resources

"Things" won't earn anyone a place in heaven. But good materials can support a child's spiritual walk.

The best resource center is your local Christian bookstore. You can find baby shower gifts, a party idea book, a tape of Christian lullabies, a prayer journal for your teen to complete, and much, much more.

Give Your Child a Bible Young children often like to have a "carry Bible," so they can take something to church. But as soon as they are old enough, purchase a Bible that they will enjoy reading. If possible, let your child choose his own Bible because children can have strong preferences on binding, color, and features. Find a knowledgeable salesperson who can show your child the special "add ons" in various editions: maps, concordance, memory verses, illustrations, etc.

Consider adding tabs on the side of the pages so your child can easily find the various books. Give your child a special bookmark to use just in the Bible. A Bible that is personalized with the child's name on the cover is guaranteed to become a keepsake. Replace your child's Bible as his needs change.

Display Your Faith Let your walls do the talking. When someone steps into your living room, can they tell you are part of a Christian family? A wide variety of excellent quality Christian art is available, from knockers for the front door to cross-stitch to wall-hangings. Let your walls witness to your children, your children's friends, and anyone else who walks into your house.

Buy Christian Magazines Periodicals offer recreational reading and timely information. Consider giving a Christian magazine subscription to your child or other loved one as an annual Christmas gift.

Use Your Church Library Some church libraries offer a huge range of Christian games, videos, and books. Always check to see what's new at your library. And when you buy a good book at the Christian bookstore, consider buying an identical copy to donate to your church library.

31 ✴ Be a Family Sharing Christ

Spiritual nurture is the fancy way to describe, "helping a child grow up with Jesus." The words mean:

- spiritual: centered on Christ
- nurture: growth-oriented

You can do some of these things today:

Share Verses Ask your child, "What is your favorite Scripture passage." Then share your favorite verse.

Recall Your Testimony Think back to the first time you heard about Jesus. Who told you that Jesus was God's Son? Offer a prayer of thanksgiving for that person.

Sing Hum a hymn or sing a song from church. Parents sing nursery rhymes and silly songs so naturally. Watch and listen carefully for your child's reaction: will she notice that today you're singing about Jesus?   Perhaps she'll even sing along.

Show Kindness Model caring.   A parent might often say, "Be nice to your sister," but the often-used words might lose their positive effect after a while.   Try making up your own family code word to "be kind to one another, tender-hearted, forgiving one another" (Eph. 4:32).   For example, at the breakfast table one morning you might say, "I'm going to 'Angel' someone today. At supper, see if you can guess who it was." Then during the day, go out of the way to show extra kindness to your child, spouse, or loved one.   Even older children love to play this game of kindness, where everybody wins.

Pray for the Body of Christ Dig out last week's church bulletin and use it as a bookmark in your Bible.   Then the current list of hospitalized and shut-in people will be handy as you pray.   This is a good way to show children how you care for people in the larger family of Christ.

Spiritual nurturing is an inclusive idea.   It's not limited to an hour of worship or five minutes of Bible reading.   What other opportunities can you use today to show your child that he has a Christian parent?

As we live our faith in many ways, we need to remember: We cannot earn eternal life for our children.   We cannot beg, borrow, or steal for them a place in heaven.   That is a gift from God alone.

32 🦋 Prepare for Worship

"Here is the way we go to church, go to church, go to church,
Here is the way we go to church, all on a Sunday morning."

Wouldn't it be nice if getting to church with children were as easy as singing that little rhyme? A successful church experience can just "happen," but more often, because of the extra demands placed on both a parent and child, preparation is a good investment.

Allow Time to Get Dressed Children always manage to appear somewhat presentable—a child's hair looks cute if it's tousled; an adult's hair just looks uncombed—but be sure to make time for yourself. After the children are ready, settle them down with books or a "Sunday only" Christian tape or video so you have time to get ready.

Arrive Early Plan for the inevitable trip to the bathroom, stop at the drinking fountain, visit to the church library, and greeting friends. Arrive at least ten minutes before the service actually begins.

Sit Where Your Child Can See Unfortunately, places reserved for families are often at the back of a church. It's tough for parents to see over heads and literally impossible for small children. When you arrive early enough, you'll have your choice of seats. Be sure your child is comfortable.

Determine Your Strategy for the "Wiggles" Young children and especially toddlers quite naturally get squirmy after sitting for long periods of time. Decide in advance who will handle a wiggly child and how the child will be handled. For example:

- A mom with two young toddlers says to herself, "If the boys become too active, I'll take them to the nursery and then return to worship.

- A mom and dad with a baby discuss in advance: "If the baby gets fussy, I'll take him out this week and we can alternate weeks like that so at least one of us can worship in peace."

- A dad tells his two children, "You're old enough to sit through a whole worship service. Get your wiggles out before we walk into church."

33 ✹ Worship Regularly

There is no better way to teach your child about worship than to attend worship services regularly.

Find a Church "Church-shopping" is common, so don't feel embarrassed to ask what a congregation offers.

Find out at which service other parents worship most often. It's not unusual for a church to have two or more "congregations": one group of people that regularly come to one service, and another, totally different group of people, who attend at a different time.

Speak Positively Communicate that church is a good place to be. Share with your child what you like about worship. Tell why you look forward to church. This kind of mental and emotional awareness of worship will set a positive tone.

Familiarize Your Child with Worship Surroundings Help your child feel comfortable in the worship space. Explain what the various pieces of furniture are called (lectern, pew, organ, etc.) and tell about the various symbols. After the service, ask permission for him to walk around the altar, visit the organist, and touch the instruments.

Attend Regularly Make worship part of the fabric of your life. Avoid the question, "Are we going to church this week?" simply by regular attendance. Consistent attendance will speak for itself.

Communicate about Worship Stay in touch with your child and his worship experience.

- Ask, "What's your favorite part of worship?" Then share the answer with your pastor; the feedback will be appreciated!
- Ask, "In what ways would you like to be involved in church?" Then find out about training or opportunities in the area of interest.
- Ask, "Which of your friends doesn't go to church and might like us to bring her?" Then plan to follow through.

34 🦋 Involve Your Child in Worship

Most churches have moved beyond providing just a safe, well-equipped nursery—which you should be able to expect. An increasing number of churches meet the needs of families by tailoring worship experiences for children of all ages.

Encourage Participation Children learn by watching, but they learn more by doing, so encourage participation that is developmentally appropriate:

- A young child can learn how to fold hands, greet other worshippers, shake hands with the pastor, and sing or hum during hymns.
- Older children can read Scripture, usher, play instruments, sing in the choir, or serve as acolytes.

Do Preparation Invest time and energy in extending worship beyond the church building. Before you leave church, get the hymns and Scripture lessons for the following week. A better idea may be to ask the pastor to include this information in the worship bulletin for other families too. Select one of the songs to use during daily family devotions. Ask your pastor or worship committee to include one "singable song" each week that's easy for a child to learn and understand. When your child goes to church, he'll anticipate singing "my" song. Do the same with a Scripture passage.

Work in Partnership Active family involvement in a church requires a partnership between the church staff and the family. Help your staff learn the needs of your family by suggesting some new ideas.

For example, ask the parents of your children's friends, "How does your church help your family worship?" Many churches offer worship bulletins for children. In some churches, a rack filled with Christian books is almost emptied at each service; that's because young children are encouraged to take a book into worship, in case the service gets long. Still other congregations offer a "children's church" area in or near the worship space, stocked with quiet playthings for young ones who get restless.

Next time you worship, put yourself mentally into your child's shoes. What is offered for him? If your response is, "Not much," assume an active role in changing that situation.

35 ✸ Set a Regular Devotional Time

Some parents avoid a family devotional time because they don't really know what it is. There are many ways to devote time to God, but a traditional devotion includes a Scripture reading, prayer, and thoughts about the Christian walk that relate to everyday life.

A nontraditional devotion can be anything that brings a person closer to Jesus. One example might be a parent who pushes a stroller through the park and talks with her child about God's creation.

Some parents and children think devotions are boring, uninteresting, long, and thus to be avoided at all cost. That isn't always true! Devotional time can be interesting and can be a part of the daily schedule everyone anticipates.

Select Age-Appropriate Materials

Young children need to be physically involved. All children need to be mentally stimulated. Select devotional materials that meet the needs of your children, right now.

Consider a Variety of Formats In a word association game, the word "devotion" might be followed by the word "book." But consider using video, cassette tape, or a game during your devotional time.

Find the Right Time Identify a time on your family schedule when everyone, or almost everyone, is together. Then simply add two or three minutes (or more) onto that time block. Do you eat supper together? Do the children all brush their teeth before bedtime? Experiment with different times until you are successful.

Keep the Length Realistic A "good" devotion does not need to last ten minutes, twenty minutes, or even two minutes. A good devotion is defined as something which can bring a person closer to Jesus. Length varies; there is no prescribed mold into which your family must fit.

Store Materials Together For example, if you like to set up a family altar, collect a white cloth, Bible, picture of Jesus, or a cross in a backpack. Then all your materials will be portable and easy-to-use, especially if you hang the pack in a hall or kitchen closet.

Involve Your Child Let a child move the bookmark, turn on the tape, find the Scripture reading, or select the Bible story. Young children especially love to playact or use puppets to tell a familiar story. How your child is involved will naturally change as he grows up. Be alert to new ways in which your child can participate.

Reflect the Seasons Accent variety and stimulate creative thinking with items of seasonal interest. For example, during the summer ask a child to be responsible for bringing one natural item into the house before devotions. You can use this as a starting point or lay it on the family altar. Attach a note with a written "blessing received" to a piece of fruit (real or artificial) each day before Thanksgiving. Add this to a cornucopia. In December, add a single manger figure to your creche set during each daily devotion.

Don't Feel Guilty Ideally, a family should have devotions each day, but life isn't ideal. Try to have devotions regularly, but just do your best. And if you get "out of the habit," start the pattern again, beginning today. It's never too late to start!

36 ✹ Remember, You Are Growing Too

The concept that a parent grows, too, is a foundation point for a healthy family. Too often, a person sees a child and says, "Oh, look how he has grown." A child's growth is obvious. But the entire family unit is a unit, and the family is constantly changing. A parent who is receptive to learning has many avenues for growth. Consider using the resources listed below to help you grow:

Relatives Find out the hardest problem an older relative or your own parent solved as a parent. That solution might still work.

Your Past Remember what you were like when you were the same age as your child. What do you remember about your parents? Thinking how you viewed your parent at that time can give a new perspective on your own parenting now.

Magazines *Christian Parenting Today, Parents, Parenting,* and a whole collection of good periodicals are designed specifically for parents.

Check out what's available at your church or local public library.

Your Daily Schedule What's working well? Are your expectations realistic? How can you eliminate trouble areas? Learn from today so tomorrow will be better.

Parenting Experts A radio program, newspaper, or television show regularly broadcast interviews with parental experts. Listen to these parents speak about the issues, and then selectively apply ideas that meet your needs.

Your Mistakes When did you most recently make a mistake as a parent? God has already forgiven you. Have you forgiven yourself?

Other Areas It's unrealistic to apply a business plan from the office to life as a parent, but some principles of management and organization can crossover to the home (see chapter "Maximize Your Time"). What can you apply to parenting from your leisure time interest, job, or volunteer work?

37 ✹ Have Confidence in Yourself

There's a terrible crisis today: Parents are afraid to parent.

Of course, many people are quite naturally tentative the first time they help a child deal with the death of a loved one. And it's completely natural to be concerned about talking to that teen about a packet of pills that you happened to see in her purse. But this issue goes beyond what's normal.

How did we get to this point, and why did we get here now? The problem is due, in part, to one simple fact: Parents don't know much about children. Some people who become parents have never held a baby before they held their own child. Others haven't had a long-term look at a child who grows from infanthood to adulthood. The result is that these people become hesitant parents.

But you can end the confidence crisis in these easy steps:

Step One: *Educate Yourself* Go to a library and check out a book which focuses on the age your child is now and will be next year. Read about current issues in child development in magazines and your daily newspaper. Ask your church to sponsor a Christian education class designed specifically for parents. Attend child development classes offered at the local junior college.

How will this help?

- You'll have a sense of where your child has been, where he is now in comparison with other children, and where he'll be going.
- You'll learn that there are many right ways for your child to do things.
- You'll become more accepting of varieties in styles of parenting.
- You'll be more likely to accept your child's uniqueness, his weaknesses and strengths.
- You'll have a baseline of understanding about human development.

Step Two: Observe Your Child That sounds easy, and in some ways it is. But observing is more than just watching.

For example, if you're watching your child splash in the pool, and another child comes up, ask yourself some questions: How will my daughter first notice someone else is nearby? Will she feel the little girl splash her, hear her say, "I'm gonna get you?" or see her polka-dotted swimsuit?   Will my daughter be happy, angry, or feel another way at seeing another girl about her age?   As the two girls begin playing together, observe who is deciding what they play and what happens to end the play.

From this single incident, you can learn what stimuli your child reacted to in this situation, how she responded to the possibility of meeting a new friend, how she led, how she followed, and what role she had in ending the playtime.

Step Three: Evaluate Your Findings
Sift through what you've learned. Choose what meets your needs as a parent.

For example: You observe your three-year-old taking away his friend's shovel in the sandbox.   But you don't intervene, because you remember reading about socialization issues for three-year-olds.   So you say to yourself, "Three-year-olds are learning how to share.   I'll observe how my child and his friend solve this situation, because three-year-olds can eventually learn how to cooperate."   You might not even notice, but just by combining the actual observation of your child with your "book" knowledge, you have expanded your ability to parent your child.

The more you learn about children's growth in general and your own child, the greater confidence you'll have in your personal ability to parent.

38 ❧ Build a Support System

A support system won't just happen. Every parent must make a conscious effort to build a personalized support system.

How to Start Look around. Look at the grandfather pushing his grandson in the swing next to you in the city park. Consider the mother of that toddler who usually sits (and struggles) with her child just in front of you in church, or that gray-haired woman with the friendly smile and great body in aerobics. All are potential members of your system.

Be Selective Choose carefully right from the beginning. You need to find people who share similar values. That's why church is such a good source. Select people you honestly like. Choose people you can talk to and who will listen.

Develop a Network Members of your support system assume an important role; you will influence and be influenced by them. Include several kinds of people in your network:

- A parent with a child a year or two older than your oldest. Although this parent's garage sale will probably be a great source of clothing for your family, you need this person for a more important reason: as your teacher.

  This is the person whom you'll ask, "What kinds of issues did you deal with this week? When did you let your child go to a slumber party for the first time? How did you handle it when your child told you about kissing games at a party?"

- A person who likes children but doesn't have any at home now. Look for someone who never had children (but isn't a know-it-all), an older person who is sometimes lonesome, or substitute grandparents.

  This person is invaluable when you need an extra pair of hands at church on Sunday morning, when your babysitter can't come and you are counting on a long-anticipated night out, or when you want a break and need someone to spend an hour reading to your child.

- A parent with a child the same age as yours.

  This is the person who will help you in tangible ways. Call this person when the car won't start and your child has a soccer game.   Or when you're sick in bed and your child needs to buy a birthday present for this afternoon's party.

This is the person who will give information.   Talk to this person when your child can't find the school lunch menu or forgets if he has to bring gym clothes tomorrow.

This is the person who will be your friend. Call this person if you need a creative idea for how to take a bath without your children (and half of the neighborhood) looking over the side of the tub.

Obviously, you need these people for various reasons, but they will not feel you've taken unfair advantage of them since you will give to them too. Your giving might take the form of a birthday card colored by your child, a shoulder to cry on, or becoming part of a family circle.

Each person will have a sense that the relationships are mutually satisfying. Take good care of these people in your network. You need them, and they need you.

39 ✳ Be a Mentor

"Each one teach one" is one way medical students learn to be doctors. Although parents don't follow an internship-residency system, each parent should try to teach at least one other person about the important job of parenting. When you teach another person using a practical, hands-on method, you are formally called a *mentor*. A mentor is someone who passes on to others what he has already learned.

There's an obvious benefit to the other parent: that person can avoid some of the mistakes you made and have a head start in learning what works.

Mentoring someone else will also give you certain advantages.

An Opportunity to Reflect Parenting involves so much action so quickly that we seldom have time to take a step back and ponder. When you talk through a problem or issue with someone else, you have a chance to rethink the situation and gain a different perspective.

A Feeling of Success When you and another parent see that you handled something well, you can pat yourself on the back and feel, "I did something right!"

The Role of an Encourager It feels good to give someone hope for the future.

The Chance to Share Your Knowledge This boosts your self-image as a parent and cements your position as an expert.

A Reminder That You Survived This lays the foundation for the future. If you coped well enough to be able to talk about one parenting situation, you have a tangible reminder that you can survive other challenges too.

A Sense of Affirmation about Yourself How we feel about parenting is often tied to what we do, such as how we juggle schedules or how many times we get the family to church on time. It's such a joy to be valued for who you are for a change.

40 ✖ Nourish Yourself Spiritually

"My sheep hear My voice, and I know them, and they follow Me." (John 10:27)

These words of Jesus can give such comfort and assurance to a parent. Regardless of how many muddy bootprints you've cleaned up, how often you've tried to be heard above the noise of active children, or how alone you've felt in making decisions, Jesus says to you, "My sheep hear My voice, and I know them, and they follow Me." He invites you to walk with Him today.

Find a Support System Some parents have formal opportunities to be spiritually nourished. A church might not only sponsor a class for parents but also provide free child care, assistance with transportation, if needed, and a stimulating program. If a local church offers this—even if it's not the church you usually attend—participate whenever possible. Other Christian parents meet, in an informal or organized way, at their place of employment. If this isn't available, work with others to start a group.

Some parents become involved with a regional branch of international organizations:

- Moms-In-Touch (PO Box 1120, Poway, CA 92074; 619-486-4065)

- Mothers of Preschoolers (MOPS, 4175 Harlan St., Wheat Ridge, CO 80033; 303-420-6100)

- Various ministries sponsored by Stonecroft Ministries: Christian Business and Professional Women, Christian Women's Clubs, Stonecroft Couple's Clubs (PO Box 9609, Kansas City, MO 64134-0609; 816-763-7800)

Establish Personal Study Time Other parents get up early to have devotions or read the Bible before the first child wakes up. You might share a daily devotional reading with your older child or add a five-minute Bible study segment onto family devotions after dinner.

Some parents refer to specific Scripture passages when certain parenting situations occur. You might find these references helpful:

- When the children have argued all day, read Matthew 5:9.

- When you feel unappreciated, read Hebrews 6:10.

- When a child says, "You don't love me," read 1 John 3:1.

- When your child gets a great report card, read Psalm 100:1–4.
- When you worry about your child, read Philippians 4:6–7.
- When you wonder if it's worth getting everybody ready for church, read Matthew 19:14.
- When it's hard to set priorities, read Proverbs 3:5–6.
- When your child is sick, read Matthew 8:7.
- When your child hits a home run, read Isaiah 55:12–13.
- Add your own special situations and passages, here:

_____

_____

_____

"My sheep hear My voice, and I know them, and they follow Me." Jesus speaks these words to you today and everyday. Will you accept the invitation to walk with Him?

41 ❋ Off-load Stress

Stress-free parenting? There isn't any. A parent faces almost constant physical, mental, emotional, social, and spiritual demands. The specific type and intensity of demand varies as a child grows and a parent ages, but stress is built into parenting.

Some stress is helpful. If your daughter didn't need a clean baseball uniform, that load of wash might not get done. If your son didn't want to earn an attendance award at Sunday school, you might miss church. Death has been defined as the absence of stress. Well, that's a quick way to see the "up" side of stress!

Stress is what you feel when you lose the car keys, your child falls off the swing, or you're coping with a crying child at the end of a long check-out line at the grocery store. But stress can result from happy events too. Consider the father who's managing a birthday party for an eight-year-old boy and his seven little buddies or the mother of a bride concerned with parties and wedding details. Both usually happy events can also be highly stressful.

Although there are various ways to examine stress, use this simple four-step process to help you: Clarify what happened; identify what's causing the stress; decide on possible responses; then follow a plan of action.

Here are some examples:

Situation one:

What happened: I yelled at Christopher for not picking up his shoes.

What's causing stress: I'm tired. Also, Chris has a bad habit of leaving his shoes in front of the chair.

Possible responses:

- I need to be especially patient today since I didn't sleep well. If I recognize this, I'll try harder.
- I can ask the children to be especially kind today because I'm not in a good mood.
- I need to talk to my husband and Chris about a way to help Chris break this bad habit.

Plan of action: I'll do the first two things now, and then wait until after supper to discuss the issue.

Situation two:

What happened: Supper wasn't ready before Jake had to leave for his saxophone lesson. Jake ended up eating the same kind of peanut butter and honey sandwich he had in his lunchbox, and I feel like a terrible mom.

What's causing stress: The schedule. I HATE IT!

Possible responses: I want to YELL. This has happened before. There just isn't enough time to feed him between when I get home and when he leaves.

Possible solutions:

- See if there's any other time to schedule Jake's lesson.
- Plan a microwave, Crockpot, or cold supper every Tuesday night.
- Make sure Jake has a substantial snack and then eat out together on the way home from the lesson.

Coping with stress is good; preventing stress is better. Use these suggestions to use stress productively and reduce negative stress:

Reduce Burnout Potential You can easily reach the point of minus energy, because a parent gives so much. Burnout happens when you put out energy and don't replace it.

You have permission (if you need it) to take time for yourself! Take a little time everyday. You might walk, pray, take a bath, or read the newspaper. Do anything that will put energy back into you.

Avoid Worry Worry is simply the non-productive use of a parent's time. So if you're concerned about your child's status on the swim team, talk to the coach. If you're worried about your child's runny nose, phone the pediatrician's office. Target your concern directly to reduce anxiety.

Make Yourself a Priority Sometimes Your child has immediate needs: he needs a new diaper; he needs to get to piano lesson; he needs to get to the school bus on time. You have needs, too, that might be just as immediate, but not always as obvious. Be nice to yourself everyday, and those needs will never become overwhelming.

Seek God Off-load your stress directly to the best source of strength. You aren't in this alone; allow God to help you. Read Psalm 55:22.

Learn to Say No It's not easy to say "no" when the Scout troop will shut down if you aren't Scout Master. It's not easy to say "no" when the timer is going off for the cookies and your child wants immediate help with his homework. It's not easy to say "no" when you're asked to chair a church committee. But sometimes, "no" is the right answer.

Invest Energy in Exercise Push the stroller around the block; race with your child in the pool; ask your child to hold your feet for sit-ups. Exercise is a highly effective way to relieve tension.

Take a Time-out The time-out technique used so often in behavior management ("Go to your room for five minutes. Then we'll talk about what happened.") works for parents too. If your child is in a safe place, take a five-minute time-out, right now. Put your feet up if at all possible.

Examine the Effects Take a serious look at how stress is affecting your parenting. Complete the following:

Stress-reducers that almost always work for me:

_____

The time of day I feel the most stress:

_____

Someone I can talk to about my stress:

_____

A way I can avoid stress with my child:

_____

A way I can avoid putting stress on myself:

_____

42 ✸ Enjoy Parenting

Sometimes being a parent isn't much fun. A family of four averages 2,000 pounds of laundry each year. It isn't enjoyable to wash a muddy soccer uniform, skinned knee, or gritty sand toy, either!

But you can balance the negatives by investing time in happiness. To help you celebrate the little things of life you might miss or take for granted:

Do Something Fun Do one thing today with your child that you know you'll enjoy and takes no preparation: share a book, dream as you look out the window, go for a walk.

Extend the Moments What are your happiest times as a parent each day? Is it when your young one joins you for a morning cuddle? When you pray with her and kiss her goodnight? Consider ways to extend these moments.

Share Your Joy Show and tell your child how happy you are to be her parent. Sharing those words honestly and openly is a good reminder to you too.

Surprise Your Child Play a game, turn on Christmas music, serve a picnic supper on the living room floor, and have fun! Planning for parenting reduces stress; spontaneity adds moments to remember.

Appreciate the Small Things But most of all, take time to smell the flowers. Yes, you'll eagerly stop and sniff the wilted dandelions offered by the three-year-old, but also look for flowers in a different form as your child grows up. Watch as your twelve-year-old daughter notices boys in a new way. Smile when your eight-year-old can peel a carrot all by herself. Rejoice when your child can turn on the shower, get clean, find a towel, and turn off the water all by himself. Catch these and other opportunities to stop and smell the flowers.

43 ✂ Limit Use of Television

A five-year-old today is more outwardly sophisticated than a five-year-old a few years ago. Television is a key contributing factor. Even very young children can witness major world events, see life and death in faraway places, and be exposed to much of what happens on earth.

Research has consistently demonstrated that violence, inappropriate language, and aggressive action viewed on television can negatively influence a child. A parent must monitor viewing time and content if only for this reason.

The television does not need to shorten the family dinner or dictate bedtime. Remember, *you are in control* of the television.

Make Wise Decisions Decide what role you want the screen to play in your family. Then each week, sit down with your child and the television guide. Talk about special programming. Use a yellow marker to highlight approved programs. This will be a visual reminder of your joint decision-making.

Use the same criteria to select a video that you use to select a television show. Work through the selection process with your child so he knows what you find offensive.

Explore Other Options Help your child explore options for those "no t.v. times." A child who is accustomed to reaching for the remote control might think it's a parent's turn to entertain. Avoid this trap. Make sure the library card is updated and the bike tires are full of air so he can naturally turn to these interests.

Monitor Viewing Monitor even the shows you approve. A cartoon that sounds innocent in the television guide or a video that is rated for family viewing might not meet your standards.

Be Creative Videotape a show to play back at a time that won't delay your child's bedtime and will be a nice addition to your family video library. Buy or borrow a recorder to take on a family vacation or record a birthday party so your child will always be a "star." Tape documentaries or wildlife features to show while your child recuperates from the flu or when he needs additional background information for a school report.

Censor Commercials Avoid kidvid ads whenever possible. Between television and video viewing, children watch about 20,000 commercials a year. Rent or buy commercial-free videos.

Evaluate Behavior Use these questions to ask yourself if it's time to turn off the television completely, at least for a while:

- Can you predict that your child's mood will be less than happy at the end of a particular show? If you know in advance he'll have lots of pent-up energy or will act aggressively, turn off the television.

- Can your child find things to do around the house that don't involve a screen? Can he draw, build, put things together in creative ways, play an instrument, sit at a window and dream? If your child waits to be entertained or consistently moans around the house with "nothing to do," turn off the television.

- Can your child talk intelligently with you about his friends, games, sports, or what's happening in the world around him? If your child's conversations focus exclusively on television programs, themes, characters, or videos, turn off the television.

44 ✱ Surround Your Child with Language

Surround your child with all kinds of language: talking, listening, writing, reading. One expert has told parents to "put your child in a language envelope." It's easy to talk with a baby who coos back, but just as important to listen to a preteen or write to a college student. Use these ideas to create a "reading home":

Use Libraries Set a regular time for visiting the library. Consider checking out books for yourself too. Be sure to use all libraries that are available to your family: school library, public library, church library, local college or university library. Visiting each type of library can open up new areas of interest for your child.

Read Aloud Read with your child. You might alternate reading chapters or paragraphs of a book. Or enjoy a brief book-nic: pack a snack and a book, then go to the nearest sofa, hammock, or park bench.

Try Writing Encourage your child to keep a journal or diary. Writing about ideas, feelings, and events gives the child an additional opportunity to process and reflect on his experiences.

Let your child participate in your family round-robin letter. A young child can draw a picture instead of writing a paragraph.

Select Materials Select books that help your child deal with a specific problem or situation. Is your child unsure about how to make friends? concerned about going to a new school? going to be a big brother or sister? Ask the librarian for help finding books that deal with the topic. Without preaching, your child will find out he isn't the only one dealing with the situation and might learn some good solutions and coping strategies too.

Subscribe to Magazines Purchase a magazine subscription for your child as a gift. This is a wonderful way to encourage an individual child in a specific area of interest.

Make Reading Memories Take a photo of your child reading a favorite book. Date the picture and save it for his scrapbook. When he's older and looks back, he'll see reading was always important.

Explore Audio Books Listen to a good book with your child. Select a favorite book with two characters. Turn on the tape recorder while you and your child each read aloud the part for a character. Your child might want to add sound effects.

Have a Read-a-Thon Let your child invite friends to your home for a read-a-thon. Everyone may bring a pillow and a favorite book or two. Supply snacks. Play "charades" with book titles. Read a book aloud with the group.

Keep Materials Handy Ask your child to take the ten step test: Can he walk ten steps, anywhere in your home, and find something to read? Keep reading materials so handy he can't help but read! Encourage reading in many forms: baseball cards, directions for a game, the newspaper, a recipe.

Write a Love Note For a guaranteed way to ensure that your child reads at least one thing today, write a letter to your child. Put it on his pillow. Or mail a letter to your child through the postal service. Then your child will discover a letter just for her! She will read!

Read the Bible Make literature a part of holiday traditions. Read about the birth of Jesus from Luke 2 on Christmas. Use Psalm 100 as the table prayer at Thanksgiving or other psalms of thanks for birthday dinners.

45 ✱ Teach Money Matters

Use these basic principles:

Begin Where He Is Much of what a child knows about money relates only to spending; the typical child understands little about other aspects of money management. Clear up misunderstandings, but don't expect a child to comprehend relative financial values until the teen years.

Provide Opportunities Give a young child many opportunities to feel, touch, look at, and identify money. Let him pay a clerk, count the change, sort and count both coins and bills. Encourage him to identify coins by feeling, without looking. Play a guessing game, "Whose picture is on a one dollar bill? A five? A ten?" Quick visual discrimination skills will help him be a wise money watcher.

Introduce Banking Teach an older child or teen how to balance a checking account and deposit money. Use the financial section of the newspaper to explain investments. Some parents like to give a child two identical, small amounts of money to invest in a savings account and money market or stock. The child can then track the value of the investment.

Explain Terminology Teach your child money lingo. When you bank, show him a deposit slip, check, and interest statement. But don't stop there: Explain the reasons you do certain things and how you make financial decisions. Let him learn the meaning of these words through age-appropriate experiences: interest, credit, savings, investments, tithe, budget, salary, bargain, insurance, offering, change, balance, taxes.

Model Christian Money Management Talk with your child about the ways in which you are a good steward. Discuss how his Sunday school contributions are used. Share your personal understanding of Luke 12:48b, 1 Timothy 6:10, and Ephesians 5:15.

Discuss Buying Principles The average child sees many commercials in the 24.5 hours of television (Nielsen ratings) he watches each week. Talk about the difference between needs and wants.

Avoid Inappropriate Discussions Immediately terminate fruitless discussions which generally begin with a child saying, "How much money do you make?" or "I saw the money in your wallet. I know we have enough to buy a new puppy." Teaching a child about money does not mean a parent reveals confidential information important to the chief financial officer in the family.

Consider an Allowance You might want to consider giving your child an allowance, or money on a regular basis. Managing an allowance can give a child the opportunity to spend, give, and save on his own.

Before you begin an allowance program consider these factors:

- What type of expenses should the allowance cover?
- How much of an allowance is appropriate for my child at this age?
- Am I willing to allow my child to manage his own allowance?
- Will my child earn the allowance or be given the allowance?
- Will I be consistent in giving my child an allowance?
- Am I willing to invest the time needed to give him the information he needs to be a wise money manager?

46 ✖ Support Your Child

Were you a cheerleader for your child today? Keep track tomorrow of how many times you encourage your child. You will be a major advocate, supporter, and nurturer throughout your child's life in so many ways.

Say It Be specific with your compliments and give verbal support immediately after an incident. Then your child will understand exactly what you praised. For example: "I appreciated the way you set the table without my even asking you." Or "Thanks for folding up the umbrellas."

Show It One natural reaction to increased awareness about physical abuse is that parents are hesitant to touch their child in public. That's too bad. It's appropriate to put your arm around a child while you're looking at fireworks, or give a quick squeeze when your child shows you a great report card on the sidewalk in front of school.

As children move into adolescence, some parents back off from showing affection. A father might hesitate to put his arm around the shoulders of his teenage daughter, or a mom might refrain from giving her son a quick hug. A measure of hesitancy is correct: It might be inappropriate to kiss good-bye to a junior high student in front of school. But children at all ages need to feel a parent's love, in proper ways.

Show up When a child participates in an activity, support usually includes providing transportation and necessary equipment, lessons, and materials. But your child also needs the opportunity to "show off" for you. Of all the people who might be watching a game or recital, only you will know how many times he's practiced lay-ups or reviewed a particularly difficult musical passage. The background knowledge you bring to a public performance gives a special depth of meaning for both you and your child. So when he performs or participates in public, follow the three B's:

- Be there.
- Be interested.
- Behave.

A parents' form of support changes as the child grows up, so before a new basketball season or the first track meet, ask your child, "Would you like me to cheer for you? Would you like me to stay quiet? Do you want me to sit so

you can see me or where you can't see me?"
Answering these questions allows you to support your child in ways that are appropriate at the time.

Support People Important to Your Child
Parents also offer support by affirming adults outside the immediate family who assume an important role in their child's life: coach, neighbor, a member of the extended family, or teacher. A note, a phone call, or a simple "thank you" politely acknowledges that person's contribution in the life of your child.

But your efforts to affirm also give approval to the role that adult has assumed. Children need adults other than parents to whom they can relate and from whom they can gain information and advice. Your recognition of that person's positive influence will encourage the adult to continue in that role.

So let your child invite the cheerleading coach to dinner. Or drop a note to the math teacher, just to say, "Thanks for staying late on Tuesday to help Jenny with that multiplication. I appreciate your time and extra effort." Your support of this person shows you value the contribution, and also affirms your child's selection of adult friends and role models.

47 ✖ Do a Balancing Act

How would your child be affected if you turned off the television, stereo, video, Nintendo, and other electronic games for an entire week? How would your family life change? (Try it!)

High technology can be a good thing. When an older child comes home from a late practice, a hot, healthy dinner is only five microwave minutes away. A video format can spark interest in family devotions and a sick child can pass time with a hand-held game.

Face the Challenge High technology and electronics bring good and not-so-good elements. What's the key? Balance. The right balance contributes to many aspects of healthy family life. A parent has an everyday challenge to find the right balance:

- At the grocery store. Should we buy the can of corn the kids like or the unsalted kind that's healthier for them but which they don't like to eat?

- On the family vacation. Should we visit museums or relax by the pool?
- At Christmas. Should we invest money exchanging gifts with extended family members or make a family contribution to a local shelter?
- When shopping. Should we purchase one name-brand pair of slacks for John or buy two pairs at a discount store?

Finding the right balance sometimes isn't an "either/or" situation. There are trade-offs.

What's right?

What's wrong?

Where's the balance?

Weigh the Options Consider the value, specific situation, people involved, cost, and a variety of other elements before making decisions. Then work to create both a short-term (hourly, daily) or long-term (weekly, monthly, yearly) balance.

Parents often work instinctively to create a balance. But next time something just doesn't "feel" right, look at your balancing act.

48 ✖ Model Problem-Solving Techniques

When the sink is clogged, do you

- get angry at anyone who's home?
- bang your fist on the counter?
- consider fixing it yourself or phoning the plumber?

How you solve this kind of problem offers a model to your child of how he can resolve a situation on the playground or at the sandbox. A parent's do-as-I-do action presents a strong image to a child.

Encourage your child to follow a workable pattern that leads to a solution.

Clarify the Problem A child might focus on related issues or events, but he needs to be reminded to identify the actual problem.

Decide If It Is Solvable Are you able to contribute to a solution? Or is the situation out of your control?

Consider Options This is important, because we often teach a child only one "right" answer. Sometimes that answer is a good one, but it can be applied only in a single situation.

Select a Possible Solution Bring the situation to a close.

You can use everyday examples to practice problem-solving with your child. Child safety experts suggest parents play the "What if?" game which can prepare children to handle emergencies. So here's a problem-solving example using a "What if" situation.

> Set up the situation by asking your child, "What if Mommy isn't home from work when she's supposed to be?" Then, work through the situation with your child:
>
> *What's the problem?* Mommy's not home.
>
> *What's the result?* I'm afraid. I'm worried.
>
> *Can I solve the problem?* Yes, part of it. No, I can't bring Mommy home quicker. Yes, I can deal with my feelings.
>
> *What are my options?*
> - I can call Grandma. I can tell her I'm worried that Mommy's been in an

accident and I'm afraid to be alone now that it's almost dark.

- I can phone Mommy's office and find out if she's left yet. She might still be at work! I'll feel better if I have more information.

- I can watch an extra television program or get a book from the secret stack that Mommy said I can use in an emergency. That will take my mind off the situation.

- I can call my friend and see if this ever happened at his house.

What should I do? I will feel better if I do something besides worry. I will make a choice. Doing something makes me feel better.

Practice What Ifs Use a problem-solving model with a child of any age. You can help a young child work through, "What if Brad calls you names again?" With a teen, you might discuss, "What if you're at a party where there is alcohol?" Regardless of the issue, the fact that you've taken the time to think through a possible situation your child might face will better equip him to handle the problem and convey your continuing interest in his growing sense of responsibility.

49 ✹ Enjoy a Family Vacation

"Are we there yet?" This is the classic question that parents dread. Avoid boredom and prevent the backseat battleground between children by following these guidelines:

Set Appropriate Goals If you want to relax, choose to visit a city with lots of parks. If you want to enrich your child's understanding of the Civil War, go to Vicksburg or Gettysburg. Put together a vacation plan that will meet your goals.

Do Your Homework Learn all you can about the place you are going. Collect brochures in advance. Find out about recreational and historical sites. Get specific information about where you'll be staying.

Pack with Care Give your child a chance to choose what to pack. Something familiar may be helpful especially at night when a child settles down in a place far from home. Pack specific items that meet your child's needs: a night light, medicine, pediatrician's phone number, extra glasses or contact lenses, etc.

Rotate Seating Rotate seats in the car so each child gets to sit in the coveted places: by a window and in the front seat. Post your seat rotation chart on the visor for everyone to see.

Be Patient Family patterns will travel with you. Just because you climb into the car doesn't mean Chris and Lindsey will leave sibling rivalry at home. Actually, the stress level will increase because of the unexpected nature of travel. Pack an extra amount of patience.

Be a Wise Time Manager Reassess the day's plan the first time you hear, "I'm tired. I'm hungry. I'm hot."

Be Flexible Enjoy spontaneity. Discover something you didn't plan. Uncover a surprise. Don't be a slave to the travel schedule. Have fun!

50 ✱ Use Those Fifteen Muscles

So much happens when you laugh:

- You release tension.
- The environmental tone becomes more positive.
- The pace of interactions is changed.
- A child feels better.

It's a fact: It only takes fifteen facial muscles to smile. It takes forty-three muscles to frown. So save your energy: smile!

Buy a Joke Book Keep it handy in the kitchen, car, or child's room. When you feel a frown creep up, pick up the book and find something funny to share with your child.

Anticipate Looking forward to something can make you feel like smiling.

Laugh at Mistakes, Not People Help your child learn to laugh at his own mistakes. He'll naturally know how to laugh at yours!

There's a big difference between laughing at someone and laughing with someone. Help your child distinguish between the two.

Respond with Humor When you feel like reacting to your child in anger, take a deep breath and attempt to handle the situation with silliness. Instead of yelling, "I tripped over your shoes again. Get in here this instant!" try saying, "Come see what Mr. Wind blew into the living room."

Match the Humor to Your Child Each child is different, even when responding to various kinds of humor. Some children like jokes and respond with belly laughs. Use kidding or very gentle humor to change the mood with other children.

51 ❧ Nurture Cross-Generational Relationships

Connectedness: That's what psychologists indicate people seek more than anything else in this decade. One of the most meaningful ways to help children achieve connectedness early in life is by developing relationships with grandparents. Unfortunately, this is often easier said than done.

Today people begin their years of grandparenting in better health and with more career plans than in previous generations. It's not unusual, for example, to track down a grandparent skiing the slopes in Colorado or to schedule a visit far in advance because the grandparent is starting a second (or third!) career after retirement.

But don't wait: your child is growing up and your child's grandparent is growing old. Use these ideas to take the lead in nurturing relationships across the generations:

Encourage Writing Give your child or grandparent a packet of stationery with preaddressed and stamped envelopes. This makes it easy to write each other.

When weeding through your child's "love notes" and drawings at the end of a season or semester, date the items and package to give to a grandparent. A child's artwork can cheer up, encourage, and bring a smile to anyone's face, but it can also give a grandparent a sense of pride in how the child is growing.

Record Conversations Turn on a cassette tape during supper tonight. Record a brief message with the date, then mail it to the grandparent for a slice of "life as we know it."

Use a cassette or video to tape an interview between grandparent and grandchild. Help your child prepare questions in advance, but each one should be encouraged to ask questions of the other. Roll the tape even during the setup and end. Someday, those extra moments will be valued footage.

Take Pictures Regularly take a photo of your child with a grandparent in the same chair or location. This will be a very visual record of how your child and parent grow older together.

When financially possible, order an extra set of prints when you get a roll of film developed. This will help a grandparent keep in touch with a growing child.

Establish Traditions Encourage your child to develop individual traditions. On each visit, a grandparent and grandchild might always walk around the block with the dog, make a certain batch of cookies, go through a stamp collection, or read together from a specific daily devotion book.

Schedule One-on-One Time Each grandparent-grandchild relationship has different dynamics, so make sure every child gets time alone with every grandparent.

Purchase unfinished gifts that will allow your child to work with a grandparent: a birdhouse kit, a pair of samplers, etc.

Be Gentle If your child hasn't seen a grandparent for quite a while, get out pictures of the last visit. This will ease initial awkward moments.

Don't force relationships. Set up situations which naturally lend themselves to sharing, talking, and reminiscing, but don't lock your child into a preconceived idea of what you think a grandparent-grandchild relationship should be.

52 ✄ Record the Moments; Cherish the Memories

The infant becomes a toddler, then a toddler with a parent in close pursuit. The preschool years are full of fun and questions. Elementary years last forever, and end in a flurry of after-school activities. High school moves quickly, and then . . . the child is gone.

When you record the moments, it's easier to cherish the memories of a child growing up. Memories are once-in-a-lifetime happenings when parenting and childhood become totally intertwined. The rites of passage for your child are also rites of passage for you as a parent.

Select several ways to save memories for your child, now.

Have a Spiritual Diary Keep a pencil handy as you work through a daily devotional book or read the Bible with your child. Jot down how your child reacted or what you talked about. Date your notes, right on the page. This will become a record book of the stages and steps in your child's spiritual journey.

Save Mail Collect your child's mail in a letter box. Your child can continue this collection as he grows older. Date every single piece. Birthday or other holiday cards can be banded together and dated in a group. Consider saving the envelopes, too. Children delight in seeing stamps from the "olden days."

Keep a Memory Box Collect bits and pieces that reflect times in your child's life: report cards, drawings, remnants of science fair projects, stories, etc. During years of intense parenting, there's seldom time to trek out to the garage or down to the basement just to save a "meaningless scrap of paper," so use a kitchen drawer, box in the hall closet, or any container that's handy. You can review, sort, and organize items with your child at the end of a calendar year of school term, but save and date things as you get them.

Keep Artwork Professionally mat and frame a piece of your child's artwork. Hang it out of direct sunlight. Also ask your child to "Tell me about this." Record exactly what he says, then write this and the date carefully on the back of the framed piece.

Record His Voice Let your child tell the Christmas story on an audio or video-cassette each year on December 25. Pack this tape away with the manger, so you can add to it each year.

Keep Your Resources Save this book or any other book in which you've jotted down notes about parenting. Someday your child might ask, "How did you learn so much about being a parent?" This can be one of the resources—and memories—to share with another generation.

Save Bits and Pieces Make a personal cheer-up file. Save the scribbled pages from your toddler, the love notes from the preschooler, the "I'm sorry" notes from the teen. Turn to this file when you want to smile, laugh, or remember. When combined together, these bits and pieces will reflect the life and times of your parenting.

Memorize the Moment When a young adult feels the smoothness of teeth after years of braces . . . when you hear the "ah" of a toddler as that baby discovers he can really walk . . . when a child says excitedly, "I can read. Hear me read. Hear me read" . . . imprint this in your memory. Freeze the moment.

Capture your feelings: Even if you write on a scrap of paper, jot down the specifics of the situation. Remember the sight, sounds, smells, emotions. Capture the moments as they happen and enjoy them forever.